How
Animals
Live
edited by

Peter
Hutchinson

*a series
of volumes
describing
the behaviour
and ecology
of the animal
kingdom*

VOLUME 2

Robert Burton

ELSEVIER PHAIDON

Credits
to Photographers

Elsevier-Phaidon,

An imprint of Phaidon Press Ltd.
5 Cromwell Place, London SW7 2JL

First published 1975
Planned and produced by
Elsevier International Projects Ltd, Oxford
© 1975 Elsevier Publishing Projects SA, Lausanne.

ISBN 0 7290 0022 2

Filmset by Keyspools Limited, Golborne, Lancashire
Printed in Belgium

Contents

Introduction, the Age of Birds

In many ways, the birds are the most successful group of animals living today. At some time during the earth's history each of the classes of vertebrates has been dominant. The reptiles, for instance, burgeoned some 200 to 100 million years ago during the Triassic, Jurassic and Cretaceous periods, but, after the extinction of the dinosaurs and other reptiles, the mammals took over. The Age of Mammals reached its zenith during the Cretaceous period some 50 million years ago but 30 million years later they too began to decline as many kinds became extinct. Today the birds are the dominant group, with over 8,000 species of birds compared with 4,000 of mammals. There is no doubt that, until the overwhelming dominance of the animal kingdom by man, the most recent past may be called the Age of Birds.

What is a Bird? Birds are animals with an outer covering of feathers. This characteristic alone, distinguishes the birds from all other animals both living and extinct. There are, however, other features of birds that are not unique but are nevertheless important. The most obvious anatomical characteristics of birds are those associated with flight. The bones of the forelimbs are modified as wings and are associated with the enormous breast muscles that make flight possible. Even in birds which do not fly, such as penguins and the ostrich, it is clear that the forelimbs were once used as wings. The rest of the skeleton is either reduced or constructed of thin light bones. The weight of the head is reduced as a result of replacement of the teeth by a horny beak or bill early in the evolutionary history of birds. The bill has assumed different shapes to enable birds to take advantage of an enormous variety of food sources.

Birds are homiothermic or, in everyday language, warm-blooded, that is they can control their blood temperature within narrow limits. This adaptation enables them to maintain the high metabolic rate which is necessary in an animal that is normally extremely active. It has also made it possible for birds to colonize all parts of the earth, from the polar regions to the Equator, because they can function independently of the surrounding temperature. Of the senses, vision is of utmost importance to birds which need rapid and precise information about their position in three dimensions when flying. A falcon can keep track of its prey while diving at a speed of 180 mi (290 km) per hour, while

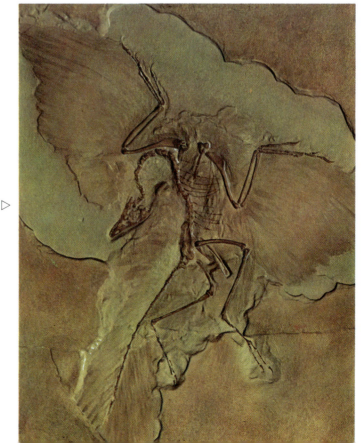

◁ An agile Blue tit *Parus caeruleus* bringing a caterpillar to its nest in a hollow in a tree trunk. The short, stout bill is used for plucking insects off leaves and twigs or for hammering open pine seeds to extract larvae living inside. Blue tits are also regular visitors to bird tables and they have learned to open milk bottles and drink the milk. Their intelligence is also shown by their ability to open matchboxes to get at food. Japanese fortune-tellers trained the Varied tit *P. varius* to act as an assistant by carrying small pieces of paper to their clients.

One of the three complete fossils of *Archaeopteryx* ▷ *lithographica* found in Bavarian limestone quarries. *Archaeopteryx* lived 150 million years ago and is the oldest known bird. The structure of the feathers are beautifully preserved and are seen to be no different from those of modern birds. Yet, if the feathers had not been preserved, the fossil would not have been classed as a bird as the bones are very like those of a reptile. Thus, *Archaeopteryx* was an animal that was part reptile and part bird.

The course of evolution in the birds is difficult to chart because few fossils have been found. The chances of a bird's body falling into still water and becoming covered with a suitable sediment for preservation are slight. Only 850 fossil species of bird are known, that is one tenth of the number alive today. Our knowledge of the early development of birds is based mainly on the fossils of *Archaeopteryx* which link the birds with the reptiles. Other ancient birds include *Hesperornis* which looked like a modern diver but was probably related to the grebes. It probably had teeth, as did *Archaeopteryx*. The tern-like *Ichthyornis* was once thought to have teeth but they proved to belong to a contemporary reptile. Contemporary with these two birds are fossils belonging to the ancestors of flamingos, cormorants and divers. During the Paleocene and Eocene the birds started to proliferate and many modern families appeared. At this time there lived *Diatryma*, an ostrich-like bird, 7 ft (2.1 m) high with a huge head. It was a running bird but was not related to the ostrich and other ratites which arose at the same time. By the end of the Miocene most bird families had evolved. *Phrororachos* was a flightless seriema, of the crane order. The order Passeriformes or perching birds developed in the Pliocene and now contains about half the species of living birds.

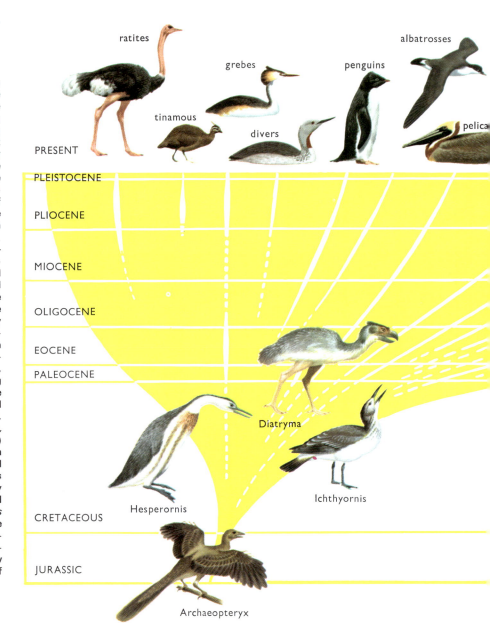

PRESENT — ratites — tinamous — grebes — divers — penguins — albatrosses — pelica

PLEISTOCENE

PLIOCENE

MIOCENE

OLIGOCENE

EOCENE

PALEOCENE

Diatryma

Hesperornis

Ichthyornis

CRETACEOUS

JURASSIC

Archaeopteryx

owls have night vision that has been estimated to be up to 100 times more sensitive than that of man.

Other notable characteristics of birds are associated with their method of reproduction. Eggs are laid, sometimes in quite elaborate nests, after courtship rituals that are rivalled only by a few of the mammals. And, as with the mammals, the young in most species are protected and fed by their parents during the early stages of their lives. The complex behaviour patterns associated with courtship, nestbuilding, and parental care are rigid and are evidence of a brain that has developed mainly for the control of instinctive behaviour.

Birds and Man. Birds are of considerable economic importance. They are kept as pets and their feathers have been extensively used for ornament and in the manufacture of eiderdowns and pillows. Of greater economic importance are the domesticated birds, such as chickens, ducks, geese and turkeys, and many wild birds which are cheap sources of protein throughout the world. Finally, guano, the dried droppings of seabirds, is collected and used as a fertilizer in Australia, South Africa and South America. On the debit side, birds are even more important as pests. Flocks of grain or fruit-eating birds such as the quelia of Africa, cause

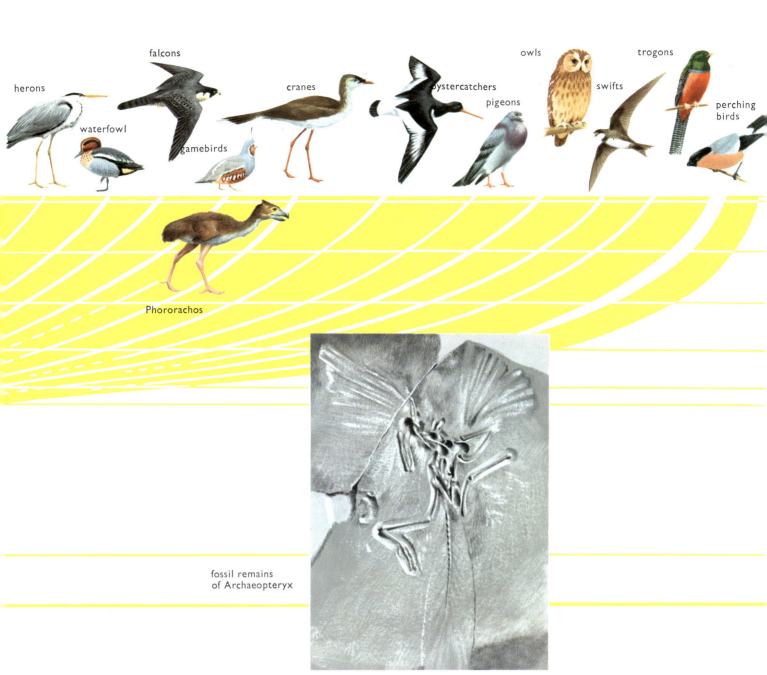

herons
falcons
waterfowl
gamebirds
cranes
oystercatchers
pigeons
owls
swifts
trogons
perching birds

Phororachos

fossil remains
of Archaeopteryx

enormous losses to crops. Birds may also foul stored food and can cause fatal accidents through collision with aircraft.

Men have always been fascinated by birds. They have taken a prominent place in art and mythology since the Stone Age. More recently, the collecting of birds and their eggs and bird watching have become very popular, especially in Europe and the United States. From these interests has grown an enormous popular literature on birds, which now far exceeds the more academic studies that deal mainly with their ecology, behaviour, classification and evolution. Yet even in the academic world, the study of

birds takes up a disproportionate amount of effort for the size of the group, mainly because their popular appeal and ease of observation makes them good subjects for the study of biological problems.

The Evolution and Classification of Birds. The first known bird is *Archaeopteryx* whose fossil has been found in Jurassic rocks that are about 140 million years old. The skeleton of *Archaeopteryx* displays many reptilian characteristics, such as the presence of a long tail, and clearly indicates that the birds have evolved from reptilian ancestors. Since the Jurassic period, birds have undergone a major adaptive radiation (the evolution of a variety of

9

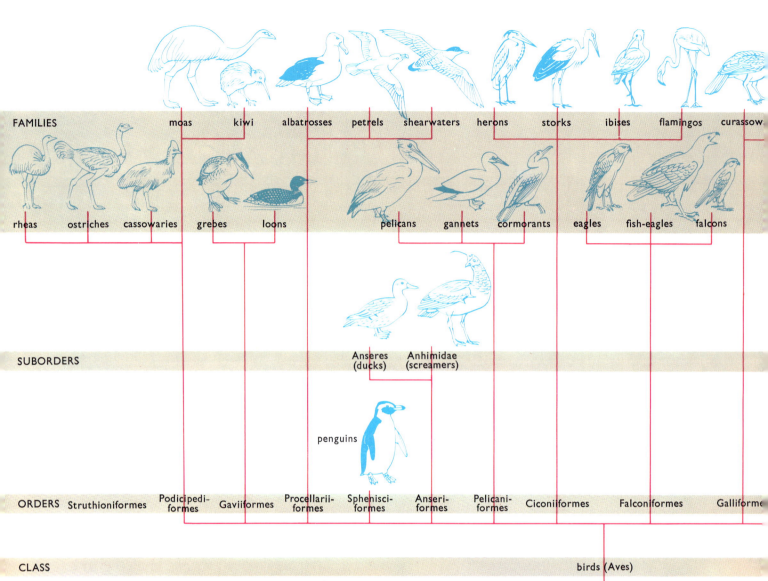

FAMILIES

moas   kiwi   albatrosses   petrels   shearwaters   herons   storks   ibises   flamingos   curassow

rheas   ostriches   cassowaries   grebes   loons   pelicans   gannets   cormorants   eagles   fish-eagles   falcons

SUBORDERS

Anseres (ducks)   Anhimidae (screamers)

penguins

ORDERS   Struthioniformes   Podicipediformes   Gaviiformes   Procellariiformes   Sphenisciformes   Anseriformes   Pelicaniformes   Ciconiiformes   Falconiformes   Galliforme

CLASS   birds (Aves)

forms with different habits from a common ancestor) and over 8,000 different species occur today. An adaptive radiation is well illustrated by the Hawaiian honeycreepers, in which an ancestral species, a nectar-drinker, has evolved into a family of 22 species which have different shaped bills enabling them to sip nectar, eat fruit, crack seeds and hunt for insects by probing in bark or chiselling like woodpeckers.

The subject of bird classification is complex because many species have evolved relatively recently, and it is sometimes difficult to distinguish between closely related forms. The chiffchaff and the Willow warbler, for example, are virtually indistinguishable in appearance, but can be recognized because they have quite different songs. Sometimes, differences occur between separate populations of the same species, and zoologists have

been forced to subdivide many species and to classify birds into as many as 30,000 subspecies or races. With so much variety, it is inevitable that two unrelated birds have often come to fill the same way of life in different places. This is a process called evolutionary convergence. For instance, there are a number of unrelated families of birds that drink nectar and have independently evolved long tongues and needle-like bills. These are the hummingbirds, the flowerpeckers, two unrelated families of honeycreepers, in the Americas and Hawaii respectively, the sugarbirds and the honeyeaters.

The grouping together of so many species, subspecies and races into families and orders is as difficult as is the recognition of what constitutes a species, and no single classification is accepted by all zoologists. It is generally agreed, however, that the birds can be divided into two major groups; the

10

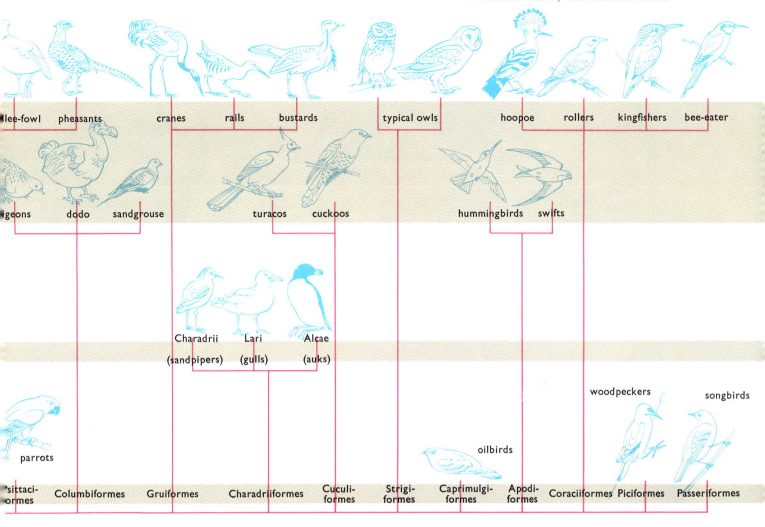

subclass Archaeornithes, which contains *Archaeopteryx*, and the subclass Neornithes, which contains all other birds. The Neornithes is subdivided into four superorders: the Odontognathae or toothed birds, and the Ichthyornithes, which are both extinct; the Impennes or penguins; and finally, the Neognathae, all other birds.

The means by which birds have become so successful forms the theme of this book, for the life of birds is best seen through the evolution of adaptations, both anatomical and behavioural, that have enabled them to live in a wide variety of habitats and often in vast numbers. The story begins with the adaptations for flight because the ability to fly is the most important contribution to the success of the group. By flying, birds escape from earth-bound predators and take advantage of food sources not available to other animals. They have

The modern birds are grouped into 29 orders which are divided into 158 families. Sometimes an order is divided into suborders if it contains major subgroups. The order Passeriformes, or perching birds, make up half the living species of birds.

also been able to colonize the most remote islands.

Birds have evolved complex patterns of behaviour, and special emphasis has been given to these in the chapters that follow. Among other topics, the ways in which some birds live in colonies while others isolate themselves within defended territories, will be discussed. The ritual of courtship that preceeds nest building and egg laying is also described in detail, followed by a discussion of the ways in which birds care for their young. There are many books that are useful aids to the identification of birds, it is hoped that this book will give the reader a better understanding, not only of their appearance, but of the ways in which birds actually live.

Classification of the Class Aves

SUBCLASS	ORDER	EXAMPLES
ARCHAEORNITHES	ARCHAEOPTERYGIFORMES	archaeopteryx*
NEORNITHES	STRUTHIONIFORMES	ostrich
	RHEIFORMES	rhea
	CASUARIIFORMES	cassowary, emu
	DINORNITHIFORMES	moa*
	APTERYGIFORMES	kiwi
	AEPYORNITHIFORMES	Elephant bird*
	TINAMIFORMES	tinamou
	SPHENISCIFORMES	penguin
	GAVIIFORMES	diver (loon)
	PODICIPEDIFORMES	grebe
	PROCELLARIIFORMES	albatross, petrel, Diving petrel
	PELECANIFORMES	tropicbird, pelican, gannet, cormorant, darter, frigatebird
	CICONIIFORMES	heron, shoebill, hammerhead, stork, ibis, flamingo
	ANSERIFORMES	screamer, duck, goose, swan
	FALCONIFORMES	vulture, condor, hawk, falcon, Secretary bird
	GALLIFORMES	megapode, curassow, grouse, pheasant, guineafowl, turkey, hoatzin
	GRUIFORMES	mesite, buttonquail, Plains wanderer, crane, limpkin, trumpeter, rail, finfoot, kagu, sunbittern, seriema, bustard

CHARADRIIFORMES	jaçana, Painted snipe, oystercatcher, plover, sandpiper, avocet, phalarope, Crab plover, thickknee, courser, pratincole, seed-snipe, sheathbill, skua, gull, tern, skimmer, auk
COLUMBIFORMES	sandgrouse, dodo*, pigeon
PSITTACIFORMES	parrot
CUCULIFORMES	turaco, cuckoo
STRIGIFORMES	owl
CAPRIMULGIFORMES	oilbird, frogmouth, potoo, owlet-frogmouth, nightjar
APODIFORMES	swift, hummingbird
COLIIFORMES	mousebird
TROGONIFORMES	trogon
CORACIIFORMES	kingfisher, tody, motmot, bee-eater, cuckoo-roller, roller, hoopoe, wood-hoopoe, hornbill
PICIFORMES	jacamar, puffbird, barbet, honeyguide, toucan, woodpecker
PASSERIFORMES	broadbill, woodcreeper, ovenbird, pitta, asity, wren, flycatcher, manakin, cotinga, lyrebird, scrub-bird, lark, swallow, wagtail, bulbul, shrike, vanga, waxwing, dipper, mockingbird, accentor, thrush, babbler, warbler, tit, nuthatch, treecreeper, flowerpecker, sunbird, white-eye, honeyeater, bunting, tanager, honeycreeper, vireo, oriole, finch, weaver-finch, whydah, weaver, sparrow, starling, oxpecker, drongo, magpie-lark, bowerbird, bird-of-paradise, crow and others.

*extinct.

13

Mastery of the Air

Man has always envied the freedom of movement enjoyed by birds and has dreamed of being able to follow them into the air. Within this century the dream has become a reality but flying for man has involved the use of machines which, as they have become perfected, have robbed him of the feeling of freedom. Modern aircraft fly on fixed courses landing only on selected runways. The pilots are strapped to their seats and loaded with gadgetry. Only in gliders is there the sense of being at one with the surroundings, for the original dream was of man flying like an angel, as free as air. Some practical person has pointed out that, if man flew with wings like an angel, he would need a chest six feet deep. This is an indication of the size of the muscles that would be needed to carry him into the air by flapping flight. Even if man did grow wings and gigantic chest muscles, he would faint as soon as he tried to take-off, because his lungs could not supply half the oxygen needed to sustain flight.

For birds then, the problem posed during their evolution has been more than the development of wings and a brain capacity to control flight. They have had to find ways of supplying sufficient fuel, in the form of food and oxygen, by improving their breathing and circulatory systems, and of reducing their weight as much as possible by alterations in their anatomy and physiology. The effects of solving these problems are seen in all parts of a bird's body. The heart is large, the lungs have a remarkable power for oxygen absorption, the body temperature is high for rapid combustion of fuel, the bones are strong but light, the teeth have been lost to reduce weight and the reproductive organs almost disappear outside the breeding season.

Feather Structure and Maintenance. No other animals have developed the feathers that have contributed so much to the success of the birds. The original function of feathers was probably to form an insulating cover for the body as does the hair of mammals. This allowed birds to become warm-blooded; that is, to maintain a high body temperature which, in turn, allowed them to be active at all times irrespective of air temperature. The development of warm-bloodedness confers a great advantage for this reason and it accounts for the great success of the birds. They have been able to colonize habitats barred to the cold-blooded reptiles and amphibians.

The reptilian scale has changed into an insulating layer on at least three occasions: in the birds, the mammals and the pterosaurs. Only in the birds has it become a complicated structure with important secondary functions. Although in mammals the hair is sometimes present as a secondary sexual character (beards and manes) or as a sense organ (whiskers), the feathers of birds are indispensible for flight. They form a smooth, streamlined surface to the body and provide the large surfaces of the wings and tail needed for propulsion and steering. In the latter use, they have a clear advantage over the wing membranes of bats and the extinct flying reptiles called pterosaurs. Wing

The white plumage of the Mute swan *Cygnus olor* is kept clean and waterproof by preening. Deft movements of the bill remove dirt and parasites, rearrange disordered feathers and dry the plumage. They are stroked gently with the closed bill or an individual feather may be drawn through the open bill. Preen oil from a gland under the tail is worked into the feathers at the same time.

Many birds achieve soaring flight by making use of updraughts formed at cliffs or steep hills. These Black-headed gulls *Larus ridibundus* are soaring above the stern of a ship. They make use of eddy currents formed by the movement of the ship to hang on outstretched wings. Although they do not flap their wings to keep airborne, their wings and outstretched tails are continually moving to compensate for changes in the eddies. They also enable the gulls to change position, easing forwards or even backwards and sideways. The bird's control over their movements is such that a flock can manoeuvre in a dense crowd without danger. Gulls will follow a ship for hours until rubbish thrown overboard offers the chance of a meal. Several species of gull are notable scavengers and, in particular, have taken to following fishing boats for offal. It is thought that the amount of food provided by modern fishing fleets has caused the great increase in numbers and spread of some gulls. For example, the Herring gull has spread from North America to Europe and its numbers have increased 15-fold in the New England states.

membranes of bats can tear but damage is localized in a bird's wing surfaces by its unitary construction. Furthermore the damaged parts can be replaced by the process of moulting and regeneration.

During the course of evolution, feathers have been put to a variety of additional uses. Colour plays an important role in camouflage and in displays. In the latter, ornate feathers may form crests or trains. Feathers are used to line nests and sand-grouse carry water to their chicks in specially absorbent breast feathers.

There are two main kinds of feather, the plumulae, or down feathers, and the pennae, or outer feathers. The plumulae provide the downy covering of young birds and they become covered by the pennae when

is taking time off from feeding, sleeping or nesting, the chances are that it is perching in a safe place where it can tidy up its feathers. A passerine, or perching bird, has 1,500 to 3,000 feathers and a swan may have over 25,000, so preening needs continuous attention. Like housework, it is a never-ending chore; as soon as one patch of feathers is clean and neat, others are becoming untidy.

A feather can be 'zipped up' by gently running the vane between thumb and forefinger so the barbules hook together. Essentially the same process is used by birds when preening. There are two main actions. The simplest consists of stroking the feathers with the bill closed, but a more thorough job is done by drawing the feather between the

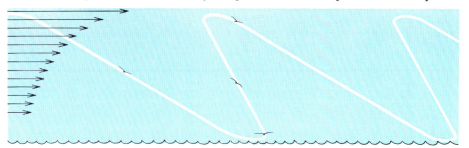

Dynamic soaring of the albatross. Windspeed, indicated by black arrows at left, is reduced near the surface of the sea. The albatross glides downwind, gaining momentum. Just above the surface of the sea it turns sharply and climbs upwind. The impetus from the dive carries it into the wind but the bird gradually slows down. However, as it rises, the albatross meets an increasingly fast wind which gives it extra lift and it is carried up to the height at which the glide started. The cycle of gliding downwind and soaring upwind carries the albatross across the ocean and each cycle may be extended by continuing the glide just above the surface of the swell (at right).

the young bird fledges. The pennae are divided into contour feathers, covering the body, and flight feathers, providing a strong but light and flexible surface on the wings and tail. Each flight feather consists of a hollow rod, the rachis, with a flat vane on each side. The vane is made up of a very intricate system of interlocking parts that give the feather sufficient strength to stand up to the stresses of flapping, yet allow it to remain extremely light. Rows of closely set filaments, called barbs, branch from each side of the rachis. Each barb carries two rows of smaller filaments, the barbules. Those on the side of the barb nearest the tip of the feather bear small hooks which grip the barbules of the neighbouring barb. Each feather bears several hundred barbs and each barb bears several hundred barbules. For the feather to maintain its efficiency as an insulator or a flight surface, the thousands of barbules must be kept hooked up. The feather must also be kept dry and clean and arranged in its proper place amongst its neighbours. These functions are effected by preening.

Preening is a spare time activity. Whenever a bird

two halves of the open bill. This may be done in one movement, especially with the long flight and tail feathers, otherwise the bird gently nibbles the vane as it passes through the bill. Apart from re-arranging the barbs on the vane, these preening actions remove dirt and parasites. The head is preened by scratching with the foot or by rubbing the head against the body and in some species, such as pigeons and parrots, one bird will preen another's head. This is called mutual preening or allopreening and usually occurs between mated pairs. As well as keeping each other clean, allo-preening also helps in the formation of social ties between two birds.

During preening oil is transferred from the preen gland under the tail (the 'parson's nose') to the feathers. Preen oil helps to keep the feathers supple and waterproof. An important by product of preen oil is vitamin D, the vitamin whose deficiency causes rickets. Sunlight acts on the preen oil spread over the feathers and changes it into vitamin D which is then eaten, along with the parasites and dirt, when the bird preens. A similar process takes place on the fur of mammals where oil from glands all over the skin is converted to vitamin D and eaten during grooming.

Despite the careful attention given to them, the feathers eventually become worn and need replacing. A new feather can be recognised by its neat, shiny appearance but, as it wears, the margin of the vane becomes frayed, the colours become dulled and tearing and abrasion result from fights and contact with the walls of burrows or dense vegetation. Wear reduces the efficiency of feathers and makes their replacement imperative, but moult in birds presents problems some of which are not faced by mammals. The manufacture of new feathers uses up considerable energy and reserves of material at a time when the bird is already hampered by the gaps in its wings where the old feathers have fallen out. The moult must, therefore, be organized so as to inconvenience the bird as little as possible. It has to be completed in as short a time as possible and, as all birds moult once a year and many moult twice or rarely three times, it must be timed if possible, to avoid the breeding season, migration and periods of food shortage, when a bird needs its full flight capabilities.

In general, the moult takes place after breeding and before migration, when brand new feathers are of great advantage. If there is a second moult during the year, it often takes place just before the breeding season and the new plumage includes the colourful feathers and plumes that are shown off during courtship. The value of choosing the right time for moulting is shown by the variations of moulting time among different birds and the way that they suit a particular bird's way of life.

The strangest moult of all is that of female hornbills which are imprisoned in their nesting holes by a wall of mud during the incubation period. There could not be a better time for moulting, and nesting hornbills shed all their feathers at once, becoming almost naked. By the time the family is ready to fly, the new set of feathers have grown. Male hornbills and non-breeding females moult gradually. Some female birds of prey, such as the peregrine and osprey, like the hornbill, moult during the nesting period. Their food is brought to them by the male who does not moult until after the breeding season.

At the other end of the scale from the catastrophic moult that leaves a hornbill naked, there is the rapid change of plumage in the penguins. In the cold Antarctic waters it is a decided disadvantage to have an impaired protective coat. The penguins' solution is to grow the new set of feathers before dropping the old set. Before they do this they build up a good layer of fat, then climb on to rocks or ice floes and shed the old plumage. They may lose 40% of the body weight during this period, which lasts from one to three weeks. The shedding is assisted by the penguins which tear off their old feathers, giving themselves a very ragged appearance as patches of sleek new feathers become inter-

Gold-and-blue macaws *Ara ararauna* indulge in mutual preening, or allopreening, from the Greek *allos*—other. Allopreening usually takes place between mated pairs and they concentrate on the head and neck, the area that they cannot reach themselves. Apart from maintaining the feathers in good order, allopreening helps to strengthen the bond between the two birds. One bird may invite the other to preen it by assuming a special posture.

spersed with, and then replace the tatty old ones.

In the normal pattern of moult, the main flight feathers are shed in parallel sequence on both sides of the body so that balance in flight is not impaired. Nevertheless, there is a gap formed where the new feathers are sprouting and this must spoil the aerodynamic effect of the wings. Many water birds have avoided this problem by giving up flying during the month-long moulting period. They lose all the flight feathers at once and the new set sprouts simultaneously. Water birds can do this because they can continue to find food by swimming and to escape predators by going out to sea or lurking in dense aquatic vegetation. Most male ducks assume a dull eclipse plumage at this time. This probably helps their concealment. The members of the petrel family cannot afford to become flightless as they need their wings when feeding. In fact, they moult during the breeding season, presumably because they stay near land and each bird spends lengthy times on the nest. The Giant petrel, a petrel only a little smaller than the albatrosses, slows its moult while actually nesting, then accelerates after the chick has flown or if it loses its egg. Moulting may come to a complete stop in some migratory species. The moult starts after the breeding season, pauses during migration and is finished at the winter quarters. The Slender-billed shearwater moults the body feathers while at its breeding ground around Tasmania and moults the wings and tail feathers after it has migrated up to the Arctic.

The Wing Mechanism. To appreciate the changes in the anatomy of the forelimbs that took place as birds evolved the powers of flight, a comparison can be made with the working of a mammal's forelimbs. In general, the forelimb of a bird has changed from a flexible limb moving mainly forwards and backwards to a rigid rod moving mainly in a vertical axis. The principal arm bones, the humerus, radius and ulna, are little changed from those of a mammal. The humerus fits into a socket in the shoulder that allows it less rotatory movement than a human arm. It is short and stout, with a large surface area for the anchoring of the flight muscles. The ulna of the forearm is flattened to provide a foundation for the secondary flight feathers. The main changes are seen in the wrist and hand bones. In many mammals, such as the Primates, there is a complicated sequence of bones in the wrist and hand, which imparts a high degree of dexterity to the hand. In the horses, these bones are considerably reduced in number and the leg forms a rather rigid lever for propelling the body. A similar trend has been followed by the birds. The wrist bones have been reduced to two and the hand bones to three, of which two are fused together. Reduction and fusion of the bones gives the wrist greater strength and rigidity but there is still sufficient articulation left to allow the cycle of flight movements. The finger bones, or digits, are also considerably reduced. The horse walks on a single digit and in a bird the primary flight feathers are attached to a single, elongated digit, the first finger. Of the other digits, only two remain. The thumb consists of a single bone and bears the few feathers of the bastard wing, used in controlling flight, and the second finger is also represented by only a single small bone.

The rod formed by the wing bones is converted into a broad surface, to provide lift and propulsion, by a flat membrane of skin on each side and by the long flight feathers. The primary flight feathers attached to the hand and first finger are used for propulsion, while the secondary feathers attached to the ulna provide most of the lift. The power for moving the wing is provided by large muscles which are arranged in a system very different from those of a mammal. When we wave our arms to and fro to imitate the movement of a bird's wings, the movement is operated by muscles on the breast and the shoulder working alternately. In birds, both muscles working the wings lie on the breast. The pectoralis, which does most of the work, is attached to the underside of the humerus and pulls the wing down. Lying under it is the much smaller supracoracoideus which runs to the top of the humerus through a sort of pulley formed by the bones of the shoulder. Contraction of the supracoracoideus raises the wing. Between them, these two muscles make up a major part of the body weight. In fast powerful fliers like pigeons, they make up one third of the body weight but this proportion is much lower in gliding and flightless birds.

The flight muscles need a strong anchor to work against. This is provided by the large breastbone, or sternum, which has a keel to increase the surface area for muscle attachment. The sternum is braced by the coracoid, one of the shoulder bones, and by the collar bones which have fused to form the single wishbone. Together with the slender shoulder blades lying along the back, these bones prevent the ribs from being squashed when the powerful muscles contract. Each rib is also provided with a backward-facing projection which overlaps with the rib behind to make the rib cage more rigid.

To compensate for the weight of the flight muscles and the associated skeleton, other parts of the skeleton and musculature have been lightened. The skull is light and bears a horny bill rather than heavy jaws set with teeth. The tail bones are fused to form the 'ploughshare', or pygostyle, and serve as an attachment for the tail feathers. The bones of the backbone in front of the pygostyle are also fused, forming the synsacrum. The synsacrum is firmly attached to the pelvic girdle and, together, these form a rigid lid over the rear part of the bird to protect it from the shock of landing.

Fuel for Flight. Everyone is familiar with the 'white meat' that is carved from the breast of a chicken or turkey. It looks very different from the red meat of beef or mutton or even of a pigeon breast. Examination of other birds, such as sparrows, gulls and waders show that they, too, have red muscles. The difference in colour is due to the proportion of two kinds of muscle fibre. Red muscle

fibres get their colour from the presence of myoglobin, a substance similar to the haemoglobin of blood, and cytochrome, both of which are molecules that carry oxygen. Red muscles also contain large numbers of fine blood vessels called capillaries. White muscle fibres lack these oxygen carriers and have fewer capillaries. The colour reflects the function of the muscles. Red muscles are used for prolonged activity using fat as a fuel and need a constant supply of oxygen. White muscles are used for bursts of activity, during which they operate anaerobically, without oxygen, and use glycogen, a carbohydrate, as a fuel. The pigeon and other strong fliers have more red fibres than white. The latter are used to give a tremendous burst of energy at take-off and are then rested while the red fibres power steady flight. Chickens and other gamebirds usually fly only when disturbed, and then only for a brief time. Accordingly, their flight muscles contain mainly white fibres, which are needed to lift their heavy bodies off the ground. Because white muscles operate without oxygen, they need to be rested after use and they cannot be used for long periods. If a farmyard bantam or a grouse is flushed three or four times in quick succession, it becomes exhausted and cannot take off.

The glycogen and fat for the flight muscles are supplied by the bird's rapid and efficient digestion and are carried to the muscles by a blood system driven by a large, powerful heart. But only one fifth of the fuel is used for working the muscles, the rest is lost as heat, due to the inefficiency of the machinery of muscular contraction. Manmade engines also waste energy in the form of heat which has to be removed to prevent damage by overheating. In most engines the heat is removed by a stream of water that passes through the engine and which is then itself cooled while flowing through a radiator. Flying animals are faced with a similar problem and also employ a heat-removing mechanism. Heat is removed from the muscles by the blood and the blood is cooled in a radiator. Bats lose heat from the blood by passing it through the thin, naked wing membranes, an impossible solution for birds. Instead, they have developed a system by which heat is carried to the lungs and lost through evaporation of water at the lung surface. When there is an excessive heat load, overheating is prevented by panting; behaviour that can be seen on a hot, still day, particularly when a bird is sunbathing. If panting is not sufficient to keep the body cool, some birds lose extra heat by 'gular flutter'. They flutter the floor of the mouth which acts as an extra evaporating surface.

Lungs and Airsacs. Birds have a unique breathing system. They have the same paired lungs joining a single trachea, or windpipe, as in the other land vertebrates, but the lungs are also connected to a series of thin walled air sacs. The air sacs comprise over one tenth of the body volume and spread among the abdominal organs and muscles and even into the hollow bones.

The breathing or ventilating process in birds is consequently more complex than the simple in-and-out bellows system of mammals, although the essential exchange of oxygen and carbon dioxide

20

Most birds moult their feathers outside the breeding season. They cannot afford to reduce their flying efficiency during this busy period. Female hornbills, however, do moult during the breeding season and, as a result, they must be fed by their male partners.

still takes place only at the lung surface. The lungs are connected to the airsacs by tubes which allow a complicated system of airflow between them. Air flows through the lungs in only one direction, from tail to head, during both inhalation and exhalation. The flow is controlled by a system of shunts or by-passes. On inhalation, air by-passes the lungs and most of it goes to the posterior airsacs; the remainder passes into the rear of the lungs and flows forwards through them and into the anterior airsacs. On exhalation, air from the posterior airsacs flows forwards through the lungs and out through the windpipe. At the same time the air in the anterior airsacs is also exhaled through the windpipe.

Only very recently has the full value of the single direction air-flow system been recognized. At one time it was thought to be necessary because birds need an efficient breathing system to keep up with the energy demands of active flight, but bats, with their simple bellows system, can also fly strongly for extended periods. Their oxygen consumption is as high as that of birds. However, bats do not fly as high as birds and it has been found that birds will remain active when breathing oxygen concentrations equivalent to air at an altitude of several thousand feet. A mammal, such as a bat, barely survives in such rarified air. It seems that the single direction air-flow through a bird's lungs allows it to extract oxygen from the air with outstanding

efficiency. As blood enters the walls of the lungs from the heart, it is deficient in oxygen and it meets air leaving the air spaces of the lungs (the parabronchi) that also has a low oxygen content, having given up most of its oxygen. There is still, however, a little oxygen in the parabronchi and this diffuses to the blood. As the blood continues through the lungs, it picks up more oxygen until, at the rear of the lungs it is almost saturated but, there, the incoming air from the posterior airsacs is fully saturated with oxygen and some can still pass into the blood.

Thus, at every stage of the blood's passage through the lungs it is in contact with air that is richer in oxygen and there is therefore a continuous flow of oxygen from the air into the blood. By using this method, known as countercurrent flow, birds can obtain enough oxygen for their needs, even at high altitudes where there is little oxygen in the air. Small birds habitually migrate at 4,000 ft (1,440 m) and may fly at two or three times this height. The record is held by unidentified birds tracked on a radar screen at 23,000 ft (8,280 m). Countercurrent flow explains how they can breathe properly at these heights.

Powered Flight. Two forces are generated by a bird's flapping wings: lift keeps the bird in the air and thrust propels it forwards. The way in which the two forces are generated are not fully under-

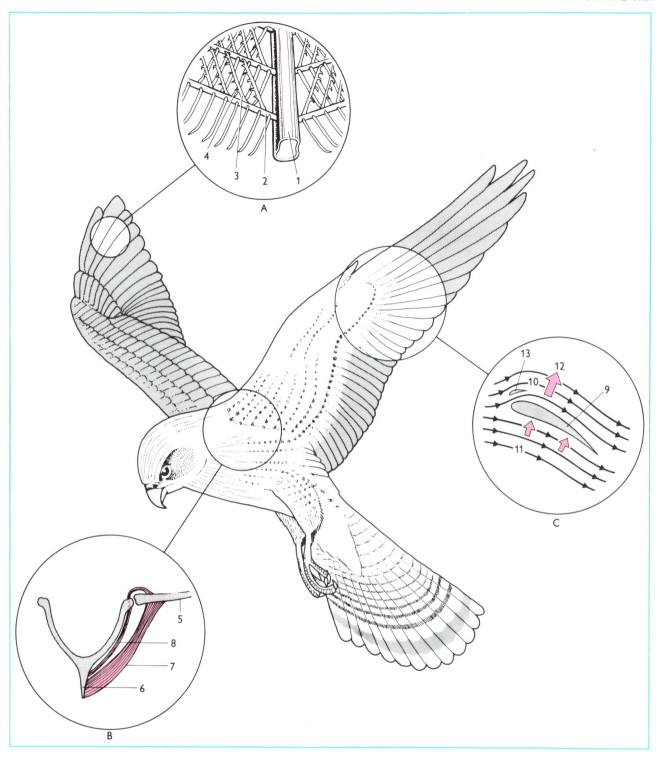

Birds have many specializations that make flight possible, among the most important being the structure of the feathers (A), the flight muscles (B), and the shape of the wing (C). The structure of the feather combines lightness with strength. A hollow rod, the rachis (1) supports numerous barbs (2) from which barbules (3) branch. The barbules are locked together by a system of hooks (4), so that the feather has the rigidity necessary for flight. The flight muscles attached to the wing (5) originate from a bone called the keel (6). The pectoralis major (7) pulls the wing down, while a smaller muscle, the pectoralis minor (8), lifts the wing by pulling through a pulley system. The shape of the wing, seen in section (9), ensures that, as it passes through the air, a region of low pressure is created above the wing (10) while a region of high pressure is created below the wing (11). Together, these produce lift (12). The bastard wing (13) functions to ensure that there is an even flow of air over the wing, even when it is tilted.

stood. They are complex and vary between species adapted for different kinds of flight. For a strong flier, such as a pigeon or duck, in straight and level flight, the wing can be considered as two units. The inner part, bearing the secondary flight feathers, moves in a mainly vertical plane and generates most of the lift. On the downstroke the broad surface of the inner wing forces air down and so pushes the bird up. It also acts as an aerofoil on both up and down strokes, lift being generated as the air flows over its surface, as in an aeroplane's wing. The outer wing, consisting of the hand bearing the primary flight feathers, performs a complicated figure-of-eight manoeuvre and provides most of the thrust to push the bird forwards. On the downstroke the primaries overlap like the tiles on a roof. The outer wing moves down and forwards, not backwards as might be expected – it is not a breast-stroke action. Thrust is achieved by the primaries twisting passively as they are forced down through the air. The rear edge of the vane of each feather is broader than the leading edge and consequently is bent up more easily by the pressure of the air. The leading edge is tilted downwards and so each feather acts as a small propellor forcing the air backwards and the bird forwards. The upstroke of the outer wing is mainly a recovery stroke, the wing being partly folded and the primaries separating and twisting so that air passes between them with little resistance.

The main effort for the wing beat is provided by the large pectoralis muscle which pulls the wing downwards. The smaller supracoracoideus is used for the upstroke, although in many birds the upstroke may be passive, the wing being pushed up by the pressure of air. The upstroke is, therefore, like a boatman bringing his oar forward, with the blade feathered to reduce resistance. It is a necessary function but is wasteful as the boat slows between power strokes. In small birds, with fast wingbeats, the effects of a neutral upstroke have little practical effect but they would be more serious for a heavy bird with a slow wingbeat. In heavy birds the supracoracoideus is larger, giving a more powerful upstroke. At the same time the wing rotates, the primaries separate and twist, and their upper surfaces are angled to push the bird forwards, so that the upstroke is not completely wasted.

Static and Dynamic Soaring. Flapping flight requires a high expenditure of energy and this can be conserved by gliding. All birds can glide to some extent, even the heavy-bodied pheasants and grouse glide after a burst of energy has propelled them into the air. But their weight and low wing area combine to make their glides of short duration. Gliding can be prolonged if there is a strong wind to provide the necessary lift, and birds such as cormorants, which normally flap continuously to remain airborne, glide and even hover on motionless wings in strong winds. The deliberate exploitation of wind to maintain, or increase, height without flapping the wings is known as soaring. Two types of wing structure have evolved to make use of this economic form of locomotion, each suited to a particular environment. Oceanic birds, exemplified by the albatrosses, are high speed, low altitude soarers with narrow wings, while, on land, vultures and some other birds of prey with broad wings soar at low speeds and high altitudes.

The land birds are mainly static soarers. They use updrafts of air to buoy their bodies and rely on the air moving past their wings to provide lift, rather than using a forward motion of the body to generate a flow over the wings as in normal flight. Buzzards, ravens, fulmars and gulls soar on updrafts along the faces of cliffs and hills, but the principal site of soaring on land is at convection currents or thermals. These are updrafts caused by the air being heated at ground level. The heating is uneven and 'bubbles' of warm air rise from the ground. Each bubble is like a smoke ring, a ring of air that spins as it ascends so that a stream of air rises through the centre.

The vultures of both Old and New World families rely on thermals for flight and are restricted mainly to tropical countries where thermals are common, although the Turkey vulture ranges from Canada to Patagonia. In the early morning, the vultures do not attempt to fly. They wait for the sun to warm the ground and for the thermals to form. The smaller species take-off first, using the first weak thermals, and are followed by the heavy species when the sun is high. The vultures soar in the centre of the thermals, gliding in a tight circle to keep within the stream of ascending air. By careful manoeuvres they can keep a constant position, relative to the thermal, or climb and descend. Their speed through the air is very slow and, to prevent stalling, the primary feathers are spread so that each acts as a narrow wing. Stalling occurs when a wing meets the airstream at a high angle and the turbulence set up destroys its lifting power. The widely spread primaries allow air to slip through and reduce the turbulence.

A Red-tailed tropicbird *Phaethon rubi-cauda* of the Pacific and Indian Oceans. Tropicbirds are related to the cormorants and gannets but spend more time at sea, coming ashore only to breed. Tropic-birds are ungainly on the ground as their legs are very short. The nests are built in crevices or under rocks and vegetation near a cliff, so that the birds have to shuffle only a few paces before launching into the air. In some parts of the tropics, tropicbirds nest all the year round and at any time the breeding grounds are the scene of spectacular displays as groups of tropicbirds chase each other through the air. Their trilling cries have earned them the name boatswain bird, after the bos'un's pipe. Like the gannets, tropic-birds catch fish by diving from high in the air.

The ability to soar effortlessly in a thermal confers two advantages on a vulture. Its food, carrion, is scattered over the countryside so it may have to wait a long time for a meal and cover a great deal of ground to find it. Soaring allows the vulture to remain airborne with little expenditure of energy at a height of a few thousand feet where its sharp eyesight can keep a vast area under surveillance. This area is effectively increased by the vulture being able to keep watch on the behaviour of other vultures in nearby thermals. The vulture can also travel long distances by rising as high as possible in one thermal and gliding to the next. In this way, it can carry food for its chicks from a distance of 100 mi (160 km).

The Marabou stork of Africa has evolved the same wing structure and habits as the vultures and the same use of soaring to travel is seen in pelicans and birds of prey. Broad winged eagles and buzzards use thermals in their migrations, rising in one thermal and gliding to the next. As thermals do not develop well over sea, the migrants follow land as much as possible. European birds of prey, on migration to Africa, cross the Mediterranean at the Straits of Gibraltar and the Bosphorus. They can cross these narrow stretches of water by gliding from the top of one thermal. Occasionally there are newspaper reports of fights between hundreds of eagles and storks. These must originate from observations of large numbers of these birds gathering in a thermal and circling together, the effect being of an aerial dogfight.

The second method of soaring is called dynamic soaring, and is best seen in the albatross, which takes advantage of a gradient in wind speed above the surface of the sea. Gulls, fulmars, shearwaters and gannets use dynamic soaring to travel long distance with the minimum of flapping flight, but it is most proficiently exploited by the albatrosses whose streamlined bodies and long, slender wings contrast markedly with the heavy build of the static soaring vultures.

The albatrosses are renowned for their prowess at covering long distances without a single wingbeat. They spend most of their lives at sea, and many of the 14 species are found in the southern hemisphere where almost continual winds sweep from west to east in the latitudes of the 'Roaring Forties'. These winds were once essential for the passage of ships between Australia and Europe and are equally essential to the albatrosses. During the rare periods of flat calm the albatrosses abandon any attempt to fly and sit on the water. Yet only a gentle breeze is sufficient to get them airborne.

Once in the air, an albatross climbs to about 100 ft (36 m), turns downwind and, propelled by the wind, it glides rapidly, gaining impetus until it reaches sea level. Then it turns to face the wind and is carried forward by its impetus. At the same time, it climbs towards its original height. The drag of its body and its weight slow it down and its impetus is gradually lost, so that, if there were no wind, the albatross ought to lose its impetus and become motionless at a height less than that at which it

Hummingbird hovering at a flower while it sips nectar. The wings are almost invisible in this picture because of the speed at which they are beating. The rate of wingbeat in small hummingbirds may be as much as 100 per second. The wing is unusually rigid, the humerus being short and the majority of the wing length is made up by the long primary feathers. In level flight the wings beat vertically but, in hovering, the body tilts upright and the wings beat horizontally with respect to the ground. The wings move forwards on what corresponds to the downstroke then flip over so that the back of the wing faces down and on the upstroke and air is still forced downwards. Despite their small size hummingbirds can fly at 30-40 mi (50-60 km) per hour.

As in many other ducks, the male mallard, *Anas platyrhynchos*, is brightly coloured and the female is dull. The male's bright colours are connected with breeding displays.

started its downward glide. However, the air in contact with the sea is slowed by friction, and the true wind speed is only attained at a height of about 100 ft (36 m), so, as the albatross climbs, it meets an increasing wind speed and its airspeed – the speed at which air passes over its wings and provides lift – does not decrease so fast as its ground speed. Only when the increase in wind speed has become negligable can the albatross climb no further. At this point it turns downwind and the cycle is repeated. Over flat seas the cycle is rapid, but if there is a swell the albatross delays its climb by hugging the crest of a wave, where there is an upward deflection of air on the windward face. A swell even allows albatrosses to soar on calm days because the movement of the swell generates a slight but significant updraught as the air is pushed over the crest of each wave.

Take-off and Landing. For an aeroplane pilot the most difficult parts of the flight are at take-off and landing. At these times he does not have the freedom of flight but must, in a restricted space, achieve sufficient lift to become airborne or gently bring his craft down. The basic problem is to gain or maintain lift and control at a low speed. A bird faces a similar problem. For take-off it needs to develop a fast airflow over the lifting surfaces of its wings and get airborne in a short space of time, while it must combine good lift with low speed to land comfortably and safely. The means by which birds achieve these ends are varied.

Much of the lift gained in straight and level flight is obtained from the bird's forward movement through the air, as in an aeroplane, but at take-off there is no forward speed and an airflow must be provided by running, jumping or by specialized flapping movements. Take-off is easiest for those birds that can drop from their nests and perches. Swifts and martins merely launch themselves from the sides of buildings and banks. They quickly attain flying speed as they drop. Cliff-nesters such as puffins and guillemots also take to the air by plummeting from cliff ledges. They may drop some distance before their rapidly beating wings and outspread feet counteract the pull of gravity. To take-off from water, the auks and most other water

birds get the necessary airflow over the wings by running across the water and flapping their wings until they get up sufficient speed. A few birds, such as the petrels and albatrosses, take-off from land in the same manner. The majority of birds take-off from the ground or from a perch by springing into the air. A vigorous leap propels them into the air and leaves the wings room to spread and flap but it does not give sufficient forward movement for them to develop lift. The airflow to create lift at take-off is induced by flapping the wings to-and-fro, rather than up-and-down, a movement that mimics the action of a helicopter's rotors. The same action is used by a hummingbird when it hovers in front of a flower. In fact, a hummingbird creates so much lift in this fashion that it does not need to leap from its perch. It lifts straight off, releasing the grip of its feet when airborne.

To land, a bird has to reduce its speed so as to come to rest gently, but it must not stall and fall out of the air. Landing takes practice and young birds can be seen misjudging their landings and crashing. Some perching birds, such as pigeons, and cliff-nesters land by approaching below the landing place and slowing down with a steep glide up to the perch. Others slow down by raising the body as they approach, spreading the wings and tail as airbrakes and backpedalling with the wings if necessary. By the time they are at the perch they are almost stationary and the legs absorb the shock of impact. Water birds can land at a higher speed because water cushions the impact. Braking is started by backpedalling and as the bird touches down it thrusts its feet forward and skids to a halt amid a shower of spray.

The albatrosses have the peculiar problem of being birds well adapted for an oceanic life but needing to land and take-off on land. The smaller albatrosses usually nest on cliffs and can take-off by jumping over the edge, but the huge Wandering albatross nests farther inland. It takes off as it does at sea, by running into the wind. In a gale it needs to take only a few steps but in a slight breeze it may have to run for 50 yards or more. The long, narrow wings of an albatross are characteristic of a fast flier but their length makes it difficult for an albatross to slow down by backpedalling, so albatrosses have to take particular care in landing. If a

A European swallow *Hirundo rustica,* known in America as the Barn swallow, flies with food for its nestlings. Swallows and their relatives the martins feed on flying insects and are fast, agile fliers with streamlined bodies.

North Atlantic gannets *Sula bassana* bathing. Bathing cleans the feathers and wets the plumage so that preen oil can spread easily. There is a set routine of washing actions. A gannet ducks its head under and scoops it up to roll water onto the back.

strong wind is blowing, albatrosses can approach their nests very slowly, gliding upwind so that they are supported by the airflow over their wings. When only a few inches above the landing point they gently ease down onto their feet. In calm weather this is not possible and an albatross has to land at speed. It takes the main shock of landing on its feet then flops forward onto its well-padded breast. The fragile and vital wings are held in an arched posture, well clear of the ground.

29

Running and Swimming

The development of flight has conferred definite advantages on birds. They can escape ground-living predators and search for food over a large area, migrating from one region to another if necessary. These advantages greatly outweigh the disadvantages of a restricted body weight and other physiological adaptations but birds readily seem to abandon flying when the need for flight disappears. Flightlessness has arisen several times during the history of the birds, among a variety of orders. Two large groups of birds have specialized in flightlessness. The ratites, which include the ostrich, rhea and cassowary, are flightless land birds with powerful legs for running, and the penguins have turned their wings into flippers for swimming. Other flightless birds include some rails, parrots, ducks, grebes and cormorants, while there are several families in which the power of flight has become greatly reduced.

Loss of Flight on Land. The order Galliformes or 'gallinaceous birds' includes the grouse, the pheasants, the curassows of American forests, the turkey, the Australasian megapodes, the hoatzin and the guineafowl. None of these birds are strong fliers and the order shows a trend towards flightlessness which may explain how flightlessness arose in other land birds. The grouse and pheasants are greatly appreciated, particularly in Europe, as gamebirds and it is the trend towards flightlessness that has made them suitable for sport. These birds find their food mainly on the ground and sufficient is available all the year round to obviate lengthy migrations. They also nest on the ground, so the principal use for flight is to escape predators. Even so, they rely mainly on caution and camouflage and the pheasants prefer to run from danger. Flight is often the last resort. The bird 'freezes', hiding itself, until the intruder is almost on top of it, before bursting into the air. The long tail and broad wings of the pheasants give them an almost vertical take-off through the trees until they are clear to glide to safety. The grouse of open moorland have a shallower flight before landing a few hundred yards away. In both cases explosive take-off and direct flight make the birds good targets for guns when flushed by dogs or beaters. A second feature of gamebirds is their edibility. Birds with reduced flight capability are not so restricted in their body weight and a common trend among flightless birds is an increase in size. In the gamebirds this is linked with the development of the large breast muscles needed to lift a heavy body into the air.

The American relatives of pheasants, the curassows, show further progress in the loss of flying ability. The curassows live in the warmer parts of America, from northern Mexico to Uruguay. They are the American equivalent of the pheasants and are forest dwellers but most of them feed in trees, on fruits, buds and leaves, unlike the pheasants which feed on the ground. Only the Great curasow, which weighs $10\frac{1}{2}$ lbs (4·8 kg), feeds on the ground. When disturbed it cannot fly up like a pheasant but rapidly climbs a tree, flapping and hopping through the foliage before gliding to safety.

The three mesites of forests in Malagasy are mystery birds. Their relationships are obscure and they have, at different times, been classified with the passerines or perching birds, the pigeons and the gallinaceous birds, but they are now placed in the order Gruiformes, along with the cranes and rails. Their habits are also little known but they appear not to be able to fly. Observations in the wild show that mesites run when alarmed and a captive specimen did not even attempt to flap when it was thrown into the air. Yet mesites build their nests in trees. Presumably they get there by hopping and fluttering from branch to branch. The couas of the cuckoo family are also inhabitants of forests and bush country in Malagasy and fly only weakly. In Australia, there are the Ground parrot and the Night parrot which can hardly fly. They live in grassland and nest under clumps of grass. The New Zealand kakapo or Owl parrot lives in rain forests where it makes paths through the dense vegetation. It feeds mainly on grass but sometimes clambers up trees, to feed on fruit, and glides down on its small wings. The wattlebirds of New Zealand live in dense forests where they hop from branch to branch and rarely fly. The kagu is slightly larger than a chicken and with longer legs. It is related to the cranes and rails and lives on the island of New Caledonia, where it inhabits dense undergrowth of

Groups of ostriches *Struthio camelus* live in the open country of Africa. Herds may number 50 or more but during the breeding season the males establish territories and gather harems of up to five females. Ostriches are very wary, except in some game parks. Their height makes it difficult to approach unobserved and they can escape by running at 40 mi (64 km) per hour.

the mountain forests. It flies only when chased and nests on the ground.

Most of these birds live in dense forests where flight is difficult except in the outer parts of the canopy, but a more significant feature of all these birds is that they live in island regions where there are few native ground-living predators. The only mammalian predators in the Australasian region, until man arrived, were the marsupial 'native cats' or dasyures and their relatives, the Tasmanian devil and Tasmanian wolf. On Madagascar there are few mammalian predators apart from the fossa, a large civet. It seems very likely that the total flightlessness or reduced ability to fly in these birds is connected with the absence of ground predators. The correlation is seen more clearly among the birds of small, isolated islands which had no ground predators until man introduced dogs, rats and cats. The introductions were usually accidental but they have resulted in the extinction of several species of flightless, ground-nesting birds.

The rail family has colonized many isolated islands such as Tristan da Cunha, Bermuda, New Zealand, Hawaii and many other Pacific Islands. Presumably ancestors of the island species flew to these islands on sea crossings of hundreds or thousands of miles, so they must have been strong fliers, like the Water rail which migrates over long distances. Once on their new island homes, the power of flight gradually eroded. An absence of predators made it less necessary and, as has been pointed out, a flightless bird stands less chance of being blown out to sea and lost. Nowadays, many of these rails are flightless or can fly only weakly. The flightless rail of Inaccessible Island, near Tristan da Cunha is still quite common. Its feathers have degenerated and have become hairlike. As the name of its home suggests, visits by man are rare and predators have not got ashore. On nearby Tristan, however, the island's moorhen that could barely fly is now extinct. Man and his animals wiped it out but it survives on uninhabited Gough Island. About 12 island species of rail are now extinct or are facing extinction. The Laysan rail was wiped out by rats that got ashore during World War II and the Wake Island rail was probably killed off by the starving Japanese garrison. One island rail has survived and is flourishing. The weka or New Zealand wood rail is the size of a domestic chicken. Instead of being persecuted by introduced rats, it eats them.

The Dodo's Death. The sad story of the dodo is the most famous example of a flightless bird becoming extinct when man arrived at its island home. The dodo and its two relatives, the solitaires, lived on the Mascarene islands lying to the east of Malagasy. They are usually classified in the same order as the pigeons but there is evidence that they may have been related to the rails. The dodo lived on Mauritius, one species of solitaire lived on Réunion and the other on Rodriguez. They were unable to fly and had very small wings, hardly any tail and only the trace of a keel on the breastbone. There were no mammals to prey on these birds and they were quite safe, laying their eggs in nests on the floor of the dense forests. Then European traders discovered the Mascarenes. The islands lay on the route to the spice islands and formed a convenient stage for provisioning ships. Naturally, the turkey-sized dodo and solitaires formed a ready supply of fresh meat but, worse for the birds, rats escaped ashore and, when Mauritius became a penal colony, pigs were allowed to run wild. The ground-nesting birds had no defence against these new enemies and the dodo died out in about 1681, the Réunion solitaire disappeared at about the same time and the Rodriguez solitaire lingered on for another century.

A less well known but equally sad story of extinction is that of the Stephen Island wren. This was not a true wren but was placed in the family Xenicidae with the New Zealand rifleman and Rock wren. Stephen Island lies to the south of South Island, New Zealand, and is only one mile long. The only known specimens of the wren were brought in by a cat belonging to the lighthouse keeper. It killed no more than one or two dozen and none have been seen since. The lighthouse keeper said that the wren seemed to be flightless and, if it was, the only flightless passerine bird is now extinct.

Running Instead of Flying. The dodo was noted by the 16th-century mariners for being very slow and stupid. It was considered stupid because it had no fear of man and never tried to escape. This is a characteristic of island birds but several species living on the main land masses have been able to develop a ground-living life by being quick and wary. Some can still fly when necessary but their common feature is the development of strong legs for running. Such birds are found in the open spaces of deserts and plains, where the long legged mammals, such as antelopes, are also found. The open country hinders predators stalking up on both birds and mammals and, as food is scattered, less energy is expended in running from one plant to another or in chasing insects on foot than is expended by flying. Thus, we find such strong-legged birds as bustards and coursers living in flat, desert country. The roadrunner of the deserts of the south-

A Flightless cormorant *Nannopterum harrisi* stands on the shore of one of the Galapagos Islands. Behind it is a group of Marine iguanas. The Flightless cormorant has extremely small wings and the breastbone lacks the keel that supports the large breast muscles of flying birds. The wings are held out to dry as in other cormorants and they are also used for shading the chicks. At sea, the wings are used to assist in steering, the feet being used for propulsion. The Flightless cormorant is restricted to the Galapagos Islands and the total population numbers some 1,000 individuals. When nesting they are very vulnerable to attack by introduced predators and they are being increasingly threatened at their feeding grounds by the use of fishing nets.

Emus *Dromaius novae-hollandiae* are found throughout Australia. The wings are minute and are hidden beneath the hairy, loose plumage. Their sole function is to act as radiators in hot conditions. They are held out from the body and heat is lost from blood vessels running under the skin. As in the ostrich, the head and neck are almost naked. The skin has a bluish tinge which varies throughout the year. The male emu has sole charge of the nest in which one or two females lay their eggs. At first the eggs are covered with leaves and left but, when the clutch is complete, the male rarely leaves the nest throughout the eight week incubation period. The brown striped and spotted chicks leave the nest when a few days old and they are accompanied by their father. Emus mainly eat plants but take insects, such as caterpillars and grasshoppers, when they are abundant. They often attack crops, particularly if dry weather forces them from arid regions. They then migrate hundreds of miles and vigorous steps have to be taken to protect wheat fields.

◁ The Double-wattled cassowary *Casuarius casuarius* carries a 6 in (15 cm) casque or horny crown on its head. The plumage looks almost like hair because the barbs of the feathers are not linked by barbules to form a stiff vane as in most other birds. The three species of cassowary live in the forests of Australia and New Guinea where they feed on fruit and leaves. Their long legs bear three toes on each foot. The innermost toe carries a sharp claw with which cassowaries defend themselves. They will attack people, ocasionally fatally, by kicking with both legs together.

Golden pheasant *Chrysolophus* ▷ *pictus,* a handsome bird from the mountains of central China. Pheasants live in wooded country and spend most of their time on the ground. They have powerful legs and can run well. When disturbed, many pheasants prefer to run for cover but they can fly up almost vertically on short, broad wings. The long tail helps to steer it between the branches as it rises through the trees.

western United States is particularly well adapted to this way of life. About the size of a domestic chicken, it looks like a streamlined pheasant but is a member of the cuckoo family. It flies only in emergency and usually escapes trouble by running, achieving 25 mi (40 km) per hour when driven hard. It catches its food, comprised of almost any small animal from insects to rattlesnakes, by running them down and killing them with blows of its bill. In both escape and hunting the roadrunner shows remarkable agility. It uses its long tail as a rudder, twisting it sideways to steer or flicking it vertically to stop dead. Rattlesnakes are treated by the method made famous by the mongoose. The roadrunner circles the snake, avoiding its strikes, and tiring and confusing it before darting in with lethal pecks.

From the roadrunners, coursers and bustards we come to the greatest specialists in running, the ratites. These are the ostrich of Africa and formerly of Asia, the cassowary of Australia and New Guinea, the emu of Australia, the kiwi and extinct moas of New Zealand, the rheas of South America and the extinct Elephant birds of Malagasy. All have strong legs and stout toes for running. It is not known for certain whether these birds are related to one another or whether they have evolved from separate ancestors towards the same flightless running way of life. They are, however, grouped together for convenience as ratites, from the Latin *ratis* – a raft, alluding to the keelless breastbone. This distinguishes them from the remainder of the birds which are called carinates, from the Latin *carina* – a keel. As well as the lack of a keel, the ratites have several other features that make flight impossible. The wings are very small, and were almost absent in the extinct moas and Elephant birds, and the feathers of the adults remain loose and fluffy like the down of chicks. Whatever the relationships between the ratites may be, it has been clearly established that their ancestors could fly.

It is interesting that most of the ratites live in areas where there is little danger of predation on

the ground – on the oceanic islands of Malagasy and Australia and in South America. These are the regions where other birds have lost the powers of flight either completely or partially. The exception is the ostrich which lives on the African plains where there is a variety of large mammalian predators. Their presence does not preclude the evolution of flightless birds any more than it prevents the existence of the hoofed mammals that they prey on. Ostriches used to live in the desert regions of the Sahara and Arabia until quite recently, and it is possible that they may have first evolved in barren country where their height makes it difficult for a predator to steal up undetected and their long legs make escape possible. The kick of an ostrich is a formidable deterrent to any carnivore that does get near, so that the main hazards to ostriches lie in the predation of the eggs and chicks, a situation common to most birds.

The two species of rhea lead similar lives to that of the ostrich. They live on the open plains of South America. They are strong runners and associate with herds of deer and guanacos in the same way that the ostrich mingles with antelopes and zebras. Of the Australasian ratites, the emu is the most like the ostrich and rheas. It lives in many parts of Australia, from deserts to forests, and is often a pest of agriculture. In 1932 the Royal Australian Artillery was called in to fight the emus with machine guns but this proved too expensive to be efficient. In northeast Australia, among the rain-forests, the emu is replaced by the cassowary, which is also found in the forests of New Guinea. The kiwi of New Zealand is another forest dweller and, like the rhea, emu and cassowary, incubation of the eggs is left to the male. The kiwi differs from other living ratites because it has no tail and the minute wings are hidden under the plumage. This gives it a comical off-balance appearance as it waddles along with neck outstretched. The other ratites use their wings as sails when running with the wind, in courtship displays and for shading the nest from the hot sun. The kiwi is nocturnal and seeks its food by smell, being one of the few birds to do so. It feeds mainly on earthworms and other invertebrates, turning to fallen fruit and leaves only in the summer, whereas other ratites are mainly vegetarian.

Our knowledge of the extinct moas and Elephant birds is tantalizingly scant. They disappeared just before western naturalists appeared on the scene to record their habits. Like the dodo, their flightless way of life and large size made them a choice and easy prey for man. Indeed, we are fortunate in being able to count any of the ratites among the present world list of living birds. All have diminishing ranges, caused by hunting, destruction of habitat and introduced pests, for example the weasel

A juvenile jaçana showing the great length of its toes. The pale blue frontal lobe or shield resembles those seen on coots and rails but the jaçanas' nearest relations are the sandpipers, plovers and other waders. Jaçanas live on lakes, slow rivers and marshes where there is floating vegetation. Their alternative name is lilytrotter and, although they can swim and dive, jaçanas spend most of their time walking on the floating plants in search of seeds and small animals. Their long toes allow them to be supported by the flimsiest of floating leaves. The nest is a simple pad of leaves attached to water plants. It sometimes sinks under the weight of the adults but the eggs are very glossy so that they shed water immediately and they are often incubated by being held under the adult's wing.

An Emperor penguin *Aptenodytes forsteri* brooding its single chick, which is carried on the feet and covered with a fold of skin. Emperor penguins lay their eggs during the Antarctic winter, when the sun never rises. During this time the Emperor penguins face the most severe weather in the world. They are protected by a very dense plumage and a thick layer of blubber. They also huddle together to conserve heat. Penguins are good swimmers. Emperor penguins can dive to 850 ft (250 m) and stay submerged for 18 minutes. They propel themselves through the water with their flippers and use their feet and tail for steering. The ancestors of penguins could fly and the penguins' flippers are wings that are adapted for 'flying' through water. The flight feathers have been lost and the bones have become flattened to form a broad paddle which has been rendered rigid by the fusion of the wrist and elbow joints.

that can enter a kiwi's nesting burrow. Several species of emu that lived on Tasmania and the Australian islands, such as Flinders and Kangaroo, disappeared soon after the islands were discovered.

The moas of New Zealand appear to have laid a single egg like the kiwi, a fact that must have reduced their chances of survival, and the male probably carried out the incubation duties. They must have lived unmolested until the Maoris arrived from Polynesia about 1000 years ago and developed a moa-hunting culture. From then on, their numbers dwindled and only a few of the smaller species survived until the arrival of Europeans. Moas were caught quite easily. They were provoked into lashing out with one leg and were felled by a Maori knocking away the other leg with a long pole. Nineteenth-century sealers also appear to have eaten one species, according to the description they gave to F. Strange, a naturalist who visited New Zealand in 1852. The last record of a moa is that of Mrs Alice McKenzie who had a good view of a small moa in 1880, when she was seven years old.

The Elephant birds of Malagasy disappeared at an earlier date. They were about the size of an ostrich, with some species standing 10 ft (3 m) high, but were massively built. Their memory survives in the legend of the Roc, for their eggs, which have a capacity of over two gallons or equal to seven ostrich eggs, are still found, preserved in boggy ground.

Very similar to the ratites, but unrelated, was the *Diatryma*, which merits a mention. Fossils of *Diatryma* and its relatives have been found in North America and Europe. They flourished about 50–60 million years ago, long before the advent of the ratites, but evolved a similar appearance. They had long legs and necks and small wings, and the largest species was 7 ft (2 m) tall. The strong pelvis suggests that they could run well and they were probably flesh-eaters as the head, with its massive beak, was comparable in size with a horse's head.

Taking to the Water. Considering the wide range of adaptations found among the birds, it is not surprising that many of them have chosen to find their food in both fresh and salt water. A number of orders of birds have become adapted to an aquatic life and, amongst the passerines, the dippers and one of the ovenbirds of South America find their food in water. The ovenbird has the same habits as the dippers but it also feeds on masses of floating kelp and is thus the only passerine

that can be considered to have marine habits.

For some water birds, the adaptations needed for an aquatic life have been minimal. They may not even have to swim. The flamingos, spoonbills and avocets wade in the shallows and the jaçanas or lily-trotters stride over floating vegetation, using their extraordinarily long toes to spread their weight. However, there have been a number of adaptations that have appeared independently as birds have taken to an aquatic life. Many physiological and anatomical changes, to which we shall return, have been needed to allow efficient swimming and diving, and, as birds have become more at home in the water, the ability to fly has become less important.

There are three main categories of water bird: those that swim on the surface, those that plunge for food and those that swim underwater. The phalaropes, the only swimming specialists among the waders, swim on the surface in search of aquatic insects. The plungers include the gulls that plunge from the surface and the kingfishers, tropic-birds and gannets that dive from a height. Gannets regularly dive from heights of 100 ft (30 m). The shock of impact is cushioned by a system of airsacs in the head and by a strong skull. The underwater swimmers include the auks, penguins, Diving petrels as well as the cormorants, the Diving ducks, such as the scoters, mergansers and eiders, the divers and the grebes. Divers and the Long-tailed duck have been known to dive to 200 ft (60 m) but this is extreme as most diving birds feed near the surface of the sea or on the bottom of shallow lakes.

There appears to have been an evolutionary trend among water birds that parallels that of the flightless land birds. Birds on water are safe from many predators. They can also escape from predatory birds by diving, although they face new hazards in the form of predatory fish, Leopard seals and Killer whales. Freedom from the necessity to fly can be seen in the moult of ducks, auks and Diving petrels where all the flight feathers are shed together, leaving the birds flightless. They are safe from predation, and feeding is unimpaired because they forage by swimming. These birds come ashore only to breed and can be considered as having reached the same stage of adaptation to a marine

Ciné films have shown that dippers can walk on the bed of ▷ a stream, holding onto stones with their stout claws, and swim under water with their wings. By using such unconventional methods, dippers are able to feed on the larvae of aquatic insects that are not normally available to other species of birds.

life as the seals. No birds have become completely aquatic, as have the whales, for this is the prerogative of animals that bear their young alive. The nearest to a completely aquatic bird are those that build floating nests.

As flight has become less important, the wings have been adapted for use in swimming. In three groups of birds, the auks, the Diving petrels and the penguins, the wings are used as paddles for swimming underwater. The penguins are the aquatic equivalent of the ratites. They have lost all power of flight in favour of their new mode of locomotion.

The wings have become stiff paddles that cannot be folded. The flight feathers have been lost and the wing bones have become flattened to form the broad surface of the paddle. The keel on the breastbone has been retained to anchor the powerful flight muscles that are now used for rowing the penguin through the water with an action similar to flying through the air, The tail is used for steering. Penguins have been timed as swimming at over 20 mi (32 km) per hour when in a hurry and they keep up a steady 10 mi (16 km) per hour over long distances. The power and efficiency of their propulsive mechanism is shown to best advantage when parties of Adélie penguins emerge from the sea on their way to their rookeries. The shore often terminates in an ice-foot, a ledge of ice adhering to the rocks. The penguins swim towards the ice-foot, submerge, then spring out like rockets, clearing over 4 ft (1–2 m), or three times their own height. As in the ratites, the loss of flight has allowed the penguins to put on weight. The largest living penguin is the Emperor penguin which stands 3 ft 6 in (1·2 m) and weighs over 50 lbs (23 kg) but fossils have been found of penguins which stood 5 ft (1·5 m).

The penguins are confined to the southern hemisphere, although it is not always realized that only a few of the 17 species live in the Antarctic and that the Galapagos penguin lives on the equator. The equivalent birds of the northern hemisphere are the auks which live mainly in cooler seas and feed on fish and crustaceans, as do the penguins. Indeed, the auks are the original penguins. The name was first used by the Portuguese for auks, particularly the flightless Great auk, and was later transferred to the similar penguins. The auks use their wings for swimming and a compromise has been reached between the formation of a paddle, by shortening the humerus and reducing the secondary flight feathers, and retaining the flexibility and large lifting surface for flight. The auks spend nearly all their lives at sea, coming ashore only to breed. Many of them nest in huge colonies, packing together in tens of thousands on cliff ledges and cliff tops. It is interesting to speculate that if the auks had found safe places to nest at sea level they might have become flightless and walked to and from their nests like penguins. For one species this does appear to have happened. Until man discovered it, the Great auk had safe breeding grounds. Not only was it flightless, its wings had become even more paddle-like than those of its relatives.

The danger of life on land is indicated by the speed with which the auks rear their chicks and get them away from the nest, in much the same way as the ground-nesting grouse and pheasants get their chicks airborne as soon as possible. The auks that breed on cliff ledges, the guillemots, or murres as they are known in North America, the razorbill and some of the murrelets of the North Pacific run

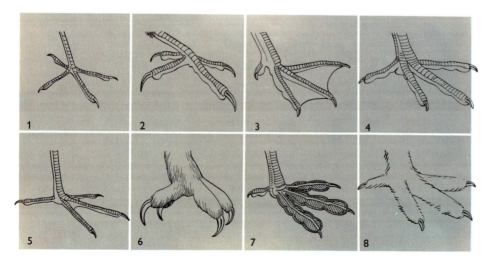

The chaffinch (1) has the basic type of bird's foot which is used for perching. The chicken (4) is broadly similar, but the toes are shorter and stronger for walking. The ptarmigan's feet (8) are covered with feathers for walking on snow. The feet of woodpeckers (2) are adapted for climbing by having an extra toe turned back and large claws. In the owls (6) the claws are curved talons for seizing prey. The ducks (3) have webbed feet for swimming and the coots (7) have partially webbed feet. The heron (5) has long toes to spread its weight.

The treecreeper *Certhia familiaris* climbs a tree trunk with an insect in its bill. It finds its food on the bark or in crevices on trunks and branches. When searching for food, the treecreeper starts at the bottom of a tree and works its way spirally upwards. It then flies down to the base of the next tree and repeats the climb. Its ascent is assisted by the long, sharp claws, and the stiff tail feathers which are used as a prop, as in woodpeckers. Treecreepers nest in crevices behind loose bark or in split timber. The young can climb well before they can fly properly. Treecreepers also roost in crevices, or ivy and will dig short, round burrows in the spongy bark of Wellingtonia trees. In cold weather they roost communally, with over a dozen birds huddling together.

A male eider *Somateria mollissima* chasing a rival. Eiders live in the sea around coasts. They are excellent swimmers and divers. These eiders are swimming at full speed, using their wings to assist the paddling of the feet. The wings are also used while diving.

the risk of losing their broods to predatory gulls and they abandon their nests even before the chicks can fly. Young guillemots and razorbills leave the nesting ledges when they are no more than half grown. They flutter down to the sea in response to calls from their parents and swim clear of the shore in the company of the adult birds. At this stage, the flight feathers have not sprouted but the wing coverts are sufficiently developed for the wings to be used in swimming. Murrelet chicks have carried this adaptation further and leave the nest when only two days old. This behaviour contrasts with that of the burrow-nesting puffins, and the Black guillemot and the Little auk which nest among boulders. Their chicks are safe from gulls and they spend much longer on the nest, emerging only when they can fly.

Adaptation to Aquatic Living. All birds get wet at some stage of their lives and their plumage has to be waterproofed. Land birds get wet in rain and they enjoy bathing, but prolonged exposure waterlogs their plumage, the feathers get matted together, the air trapped in the feathers is lost, so ruining the insulating capacity, and the bird may die of exposure. It will also sink because the trapped air contributes much of its buoyancy.

Waterlogging is prevented in all but extreme soaking by the waterproof properties of the feathers. Waterproofing is produced by the fine structure of the feathers. The microscopic spacing of the barbs and barbules traps air in each feather, making a physical barrier impervious to water. The barrier is broken down by contamination with oil, detergents, droppings or other dirt and is maintained by preening. Preen oil acts as a seal or varnish setting the fine structure of the feathers, and has only a secondary water-repelling action of its own. Its importance in maintaining waterproofing is shown by the large size of preen glands in water birds, while the frigate bird, which gets waterlogged in a rainstorm and cannot alight on the sea, has only a small gland. One of the enigmas of ornithology is that cormorants and darters get waterlogged easily. In other respects they are very well adapted to an aquatic life but after emerging from the water they hold their wings out to dry.

Buoyancy is also supplied by the airsacs that ramify throughout the body. They effectively reduce the weight of a given volume of bird. The diving birds have smaller airsacs than others, which, no doubt, helps them to stay submerged. The buoyancy due to air trapped in the feathers can be varied by the grebes, divers and darters. They 'blow their tanks' like a submarine, by pressing the feathers against the body to squeeze out air, thus they are able to submerge until only their heads and necks are showing.

Further adaptations to an aquatic life include the webbing of the feet and the position of the legs at the rear of the body. The latter has been taken to extremes in the divers and some petrels, which move on land by shuffling on their breasts, and in

The shag or Green cormorant *Phalacrocorax aristotelis* of European coasts avoids competition with the Common cormorant by feeding in deeper water and concentrating on smaller fish. Fish are chased underwater and grasped in the slender, hooked bill. Like other members of the order Pelecaniformes, which includes the pelicans, gannets and darters, all four toes are joined by a web. Propulsion for swimming is achieved with the feet, the wings and tail helping in braking and steering. The cormorant family is peculiar in that the wings are not fully waterproofed, a feature it shares with the related darters. After swimming, a cormorant will perch with its wings outstretched to dry. The shag is less prone to this behaviour than some other cormorants. In the Far East the Common and Temminck's cormorants are trained to catch fish. The fisherman has a small flock of cormorants which may be tethered with a long cord or free ranging. Each bird has a metal ring around its neck so that it cannot swallow large fish. On its return to the boat, the cormorant is relieved of its fish and rewarded with a small piece of fish. Cormorant fishing dates back to the 12th century in China and Japan and it was once practised in England.

The Secretary bird *Sagittarius serpentarius* is an unusual bird of prey that looks more like a crane and has a terrestrial way of life. It lives in the grasslands of Africa, preferring areas of short grass where it strides about looking for food. Like other terrestrial, running birds, the Secretary bird has short toes. It stamps to flush small animals which it seizes with its bill. It has to carry food to its chicks in its bill as it cannot grasp with its feet as do other birds of prey. The main food consists of rodents and insects but many reptiles are also taken. Secretary birds have earned a good reputation for killing snakes, which they despatch by trampling underfoot. Secretary birds can fly well, although they need a run to take-off. Once airborne they can soar in thermals, like vultures, sometimes attaining good heights. The courtship display takes place in the air and Secretary birds sometimes move great distances to converge on plagues of locusts or rodents. The Secretary bird gets its name from the resemblance of its scant crest of black feathers to the quill pens which 18th century clerks stuck in their wigs.

the auks and penguins which stand upright. The use of the wings for swimming has already been mentioned. Apart from the auks, penguins and diving petrels which regularly swim with paddle-like wings, the kingfishers and dippers use their wings for swimming and the cormorants and some ducks use theirs for steering underwater and for giving an extra boost when diving.

Individual and Social Behaviour

For a long time the birds have been dismissed as unintelligent and their actions have been thought of as being driven by 'blind instinct'. Casual observations reinforced this idea, as anyone who has tried to get a chicken back into its run will know. The chicken clearly wants to be reunited with the other chickens but it persists in running up and down the wire and refusing to go through the hole that has been specially left for it. But in the last few years it has been discovered that instinctive behaviour is not as totally rigid as was thought. It can be modified through experience and birds may even show signs of true intelligence.

The first experiments on bird behaviour supported the idea that bird behaviour is mainly instinctive: that in a given situation a bird reacts with a set train of behaviour without any appreciation of the situation. One of the best known experiments on bird behaviour has been described by David Lack in *The Life of the Robin*. He had observed the way in which rival European robins threaten one another by showing off their red breasts and sought to investigate their behaviour further by presenting them with a stuffed robin. Their reactions were unexpectedly violent. The stuffed robin was buffeted repeatedly and eventually its head came off, but the attacks continued. Next, the stuffed robin was progressively mutilated until it was found that the robins would still attack when there was nothing more than a bunch of red feathers wired to a branch. Now, it is known that birds have very good eyesight so, if they had any intelligence,

A flock of budgerigars *Melopsittacus undulatus* gathers at a waterhole. Budgerigars are small, long-tailed parrots that live in the drier parts of Australia. They eat seeds and, although they can go a long time without water, the flocks often visit waterholes. Budgerigars live in flocks throughout the year. They nest in colonies, each pair laying its eggs in a hole in an old tree. One tree may be occupied by several pairs of budgerigars. Outside the breeding season the flocks become nomadic. They roam the country in search of food and water. In particularly dry years they may have to travel many miles. Many seed-eating birds live in flocks. By moving about together they can make the best use of a crop of seeds, stripping the plants as they ripen, then moving to a new crop. These birds are often pests because flocks descend on agricultural seed crops.

Fischer's lovebird *Agapornis fischeri*. Lovebirds are small African parrots related to the Hanging parrots or Bat parrots of Asia. Lovebirds are so named because of the way a pair will spend much of the time huddled together. Hanging parrots are named after their habit of roosting upside down, hanging by the feet from branches.

the robins must have been aware that they were not attacking a real robin. Clearly 'blind instinct' was leading them to attack anything resembling the red breast of a rival.

Similar stupidity and failure to appreciate the true situation is shown by the Wandering albatross. It lays its single egg in a huge nest of moss and earth. If this is removed, the albatross does not seem unduly worried. It takes a little longer to settle down, but it soon relaxes. If the human observer indulges in anthropomorphic fancies, he sees the albatross as first betraying some perplexity as it settles on the empty nest but finally shrugging its shoulders as if explaining to itself that its orders are to sit on the nest until relieved, but not to reason why.

Instinct and the Brain. A basis for lack of intelligence in birds was apparently discovered when anatomists dissected the brains of birds and compared them with the brains of mammals. In mammals the seat of intelligence is the cerebral cortex, the outer covering of the paired cerebral hemispheres. By and large, the larger the area of cerebral cortex, the more intelligent is the mammal. The large cerebral cortex of man and the dolphins has an increased surface area through being thrown into folds or convolutions. At the other end of the scale, the cerebral cortex of insectivores and marsupials is small and smooth. In the birds, the cerebral hemispheres are quite large but the cortex is hardly more developed than in reptiles. The size of the hemispheres is due to the enlargement of the underlying tissue, the corpus striatum. The corpus striatum was supposed to be solely concerned with instinctive behaviour and its development in birds tied in nicely with what was known of their behaviour, that it was mainly instinctive. It is now known that this interpretation is incorrect. The birds and mammals evolved from the reptiles separately so they cannot be directly compared. The only characters they have in common are those that can be traced to a common reptilian ancestor. Thus, in the evolution of the brain, the reptiles started to develop the lower part of the corpus striatum. When the mammals arose, they concentrated on developing the cortex. The birds continued to develop the corpus striatum, principally as a site for the control of 'instinctive' actions, but a part of it, called the hyperstriatum, was set aside as a seat of learning. It was the significance of the hyperstriatum which was missed by the early anatomists.

The experiment with the robin and the deception of the Wandering albatross are examples of bird behaviour which are unfair to birds. Under normal circumstances robins meet red feathers on living robins and albatross eggs do not suddenly vanish.

46

It is man the experimenter who has been making the situation unreal; the birds are quite able to cope with naturally occurring circumstances. This is the crux of the matter. Instinctive behaviour enables an animal to cope with the normal problems of life, the changes in its environment and interactions with other animals, whether they be prey, predators, mates or offspring. Only when abnormal problems arise does instinctive behaviour reveal its failings. A shortage of food, severe weather or a new enemy can destroy a species. The dodo died so easily because it had no instinctive reaction to run away from man and his domestic animals. The drawback to instinctive behaviour is that it can only change through the process of natural selection, which was too slow to help the dodo.

Analysing Instinct. Instinctive behaviour is relatively simple and rigid. Each behaviour pattern is inherited, so that an animal is born with a set of behaviour programmes that are set in motion under the correct circumstances. The programme can be summarized very simply as, stimulus – nervous mechanism – response. The tuft of red feathers wired to a branch is a stimulus, the robin's threats and attacks are a response to it. The response can be altered by varying the form of the stimulus and by doing this systematically and progressively, one can gain an insight into the nature of the nervous mechanism of the behaviour pattern. The experimental study of behaviour along these lines has proved very fruitful. It has formed the basis for theories of brain mechanism and, perhaps more successfully, has shown how an animal's behaviour is so organized as to work with optimum efficiency and simplicity.

A Herring gull chick solicits food by pecking at the tip of its parent's bill. In response, the parent regurgitates a small mass of food and holds it in its bill for the chick to eat. The shape and colour of the parent's bill is the stimulus that initiates this feeding behaviour, together with an internal hunger drive, so there is a simple mechanism whereby a chick is fed when it is hungry. In a series of experiments, Herring gull chicks were hatched in an incubator and presented with artificial bills of various sizes and colours. The effectiveness of the different models was measured by counting the number of pecks each model received during a given period. The conclusion was that the best bill is long, thin and red. It has to be moving and held in a vertical position not far from the chick's head. In many respects this is the natural stimulus that a Herring gull presents to its chick. It holds its bill vertically; it is usually moving and there is a red spot at the tip of the bill.

The interpretation of the experimental results is, however, not quite straightforward. The chicks preferred to peck at red than at any other colour and the question is whether they prefer red because the parent has a red spot on its bill or whether the red spot evolved because the chicks prefer to peck at red? The answer seems to be that the chicks can see red better than other colours, so that the evolution of the red spot made the bill a conspicuous target.

A second feature of the pecking tests is that the chick preferred some models to the real bill. They prefer a long, narrow model to one the same size as a Herring gull's bill, and they prefer a wholly red bill to a yellow one with a red spot. Such stimuli which evoke a stronger than normal response are called supernormal stimuli. Their existence shows

The bullfinch *Pyrrhula pyrrhula,* a beautiful bird that becomes a pest when it strips buds in orchards. It lives in the cover of trees and bushes and its presence is often first realized by its soft piping song. The bullfinch, unlike some other birds, has to learn its song. In the wild, it copies other bullfinches, but captive bullfinches can be trained to copy other sounds. At one time bullfinches were kept at bird-schools in Central Europe where they were trained by means of a bird flageolet. There is a report, before World War I, of a German bullfinch that could whistle the British National Anthem.

European starlings *Sturnus vulgaris* gathering at a roost that may contain over a million individuals.

that the animal has not evolved the optimum stimulus and response interaction. This is because a compromise has been necessary. A gull's bill has more functions than that of stimulating pecking by chicks. Its principal function is catching food and a gull's bill is a good shape for catching fish and other small animals. Furthermore, the bill's colour serves other purposes: it acts as a signal between adults as well as between adult and chick. A bill is, therefore, a compromise organ that carries out each of several functions adequately.

Supernormal stimuli are mainly experimental oddities. Oystercatchers will, for example, prefer to sit on a huge model egg than on one of their own. In a few cases, however, supernormal stimuli have been turned to good use, as in the way that cuckoos make use of the gaping behaviour of young birds. In many small birds the brightly coloured mouth of the nestling is a stimulus for the parents' to place food in it. Fledgling cuckoos have capitalized on this and they divert passing birds from feeding their own offspring to putting food into a mouth so large that the adult bird could almost disappear inside.

Clever Birds. Experiments on bird behaviour have brought about a fundamental change in our ideas on the mechanism of behaviour in general. At one time it was thought that instinct and learning were completely separate forms of behaviour. Instinct was said to be hereditary and rigid: a set stimulus always evoking a set response. Learning on the other hand, was known to be flexible: by learning, an animal can benefit from its mistakes, instead of continuing to make them. It can adapt to changing circumstances and increase its chances of survival. Learning was, therefore, said to be a more advanced form of behaviour and an animal that can learn was more advanced than one bound by the traditions of instinct. It is now realized that instinctive behaviour can be just as advantageous to an animal as learning. It is also realized that the two forms of behaviour are often linked and that learning plays a larger part in the life of birds than was supposed.

A learning process is often superimposed on an instinct so that the hereditary patterns of behaviour correct for the survival of the species can be modified to fit the particular circumstances of the

48

individual. A few examples will illustrate this. The young of domestic chicks have to feed themselves from the moment that they hatch. They instinctively peck at anything that is small and contrasts with the ground underneath, but by a process of trial and error they learn to peck only at objects that are edible. It is clear that a chick has to have the instinctive ability to feed itself but, unless it is able to learn what objects are inedible and leave them alone, it will waste considerable time and effort.

Another instinctive piece of behaviour is flying. When it is time to leave the nest, young pigeons reared with their wings securely but safely held against their bodies fly as well as pigeons that have been able to exercise their wings. In fact, many birds grow up in holes or burrows where there is no room for exercise. Flying is, therefore, instinctive but learning is needed for the fine control of flight, particularly at landing. If flying had to be learnt as a child has to learn to ride a bicycle, few birds would get far from their nests before coming to grief.

Finally, by rearing birds in strict isolation it has been found that some birds have to learn to sing. Cuckoos, whitethroats and Reed buntings sing instinctively, the full song being developed per-fectly by birds reared in isolation. Bullfinches have to learn their songs by listening to other bullfinches and a bullfinch that grew up with a canary sang like a canary. Chaffinches and Song sparrows have a basic song that is hereditary but they have to hear other males of their own species in order to develop variations on this basic theme.

As the study of bird behaviour has developed, it has become clear that not only do birds regularly make use of a capacity to learn to improve their basically instinctive activities, such as feeding, nest-building and singing, but that this capacity extends beyond mere trial and error learning. Birds are often quite clever; they can solve problems and show signs of reasoning. There are several records of birds using remarkable intelligence in the wild. It has been recorded in Scandinavia that Hooded crows have learnt to steal fish from lines which are set through holes in the ice by the fishermen. The crows learnt to draw in the lines and seize the fish from the hooks. This requires more than just grabbing the line and walking backwards until the fish surface. The crows have to walk back to the hole, keeping their feet on the line so that the fish does not slip back into the water.

Golden weavers *Ploceus castaneiceps.* nest in colonies and feed in flocks. Their broad wedge-shaped bills show that these birds are seed eaters.

An oystercatcher *Haematopus ostralegus* attempting to sit on a giant model of an egg in preference to its own and that of a gull. The oystercatcher instinctively sits on eggs during the breeding season. The sight of eggs in the nest is the stimulus or trigger causing the oystercatcher to respond with incubation behaviour. The outsize egg constitutes a supernormal stimulus which elicits a stronger response than does the natural stimulus.

There is an isolated record of an American Green heron that formed the habit of using pieces of bread as bait. It would drop the bread into the water and catch little fish as they came to nibble it. It even drove away other birds that tried to eat the bread. As this is the only record of a Green heron behaving in such a way, this individual must have been a genius among herons. Presumably, it was intelligent enough to connect the presence of a floating piece of bread with fish, and then to search for its own pieces. The trick must have made life quite easy for it as an individual but was of no longstanding advantage to the species.

To be of use to the species a new trick has to be transmitted to other individuals and from one generation to another by imitative learning. Some British tits learned to open milk bottles and steal the milk. Their companions copied them and the habit has spread across the country. Rather similar was the spread of a particular feeding habit among

Experiments with gulls and robins show that the behaviour of a bird consists of responses to particular stimulae. A Herring gull chick demands food by pecking at its parent's bill. In (A), a chick reared in an incubator is presented with a red model of its parents bill, and is seen to respond in the normal way. There is no response to a bill of identical shape which lacks red colouration (B). In real life (C), a small red spot on the parents bill is enough to stimulate the begging response. The European robin will attack any model so long as it contains some red colouration (D), but will ignore an almost perfect model of another robin (E). These results are explained by the fact that the male European robin has a red breast (F), and it is the red colour, not the shape of the bird, that stimulates a response to a potential rival.

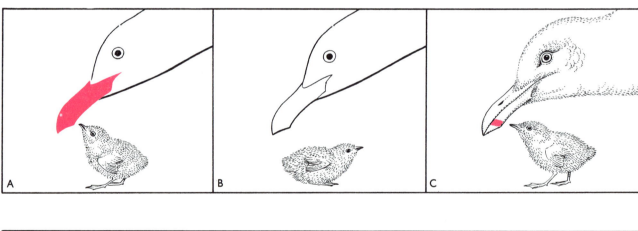

Pelicans roosting on the plains of East Africa. The larger pelicans roost on the ground but smaller species seek the safety of the trees.

greenfinches. Their main food is seeds and one or two centuries ago greenfinches living in the north of England developed a passion for the seeds of *Daphne meyereum*, a shrub that flowers in February and March and is grown in gardens for its fragrant blossom. The seeds ripen in mid June and the greenfinches, which have been keeping watch on them, strip the bushes clean. The habit of stripping *Daphne* bushes has been spreading from the north of England at the rate of $1\frac{1}{4}$–$2\frac{1}{2}$ mi (2–4 km) per year. It has now spread through most of the British Isles and has crossed to continental Europe.

We can infer that tits and greenfinches learn these special feeding habits from their companions but it does not tell us much about their learning ability or intelligence. We do not know whether these birds are learning by laborious trial and error or whether they are showing insight into problems. Solving a problem by insight is a sign of high intelligence but it is not easy to design intelligence tests for birds.

Can Birds Count? A sure sign of intelligence is the ability to count and, in this respect, it would seem that birds are not well endowed. Counting

experiments with birds often take the form of presenting a bird with a card bearing a number of dots. The bird has to pick up the same number of lumps of food or 'baits' from a selection scattered on the floor or contained in boxes. In one such experiment a jackdaw had to lift the lids off boxes and remove five baits. Some boxes contained no bait, others contained one or two baits. Thus, it had to open the boxes in an orderly sequence and count the baits that it ate. On one occasion, the jackdaw opened three boxes and took one bait from the first and third and two from the second. It then retired to its cage, having scored a failure by taking only four baits. But, before the experimenter could record this, the jackdaw came back and 'bowed' before the open boxes. It bowed once in front of the first box, twice in front of the second and once in front of the third. Then it opened more boxes until it found another bait, the fifth. Having done this, it returned to its cage once more.

There must have been quite a series of activities going on inside this jackdaw's mind. First, it realized that it had made a mistake and then that it ought to go back and correct it. This is thought on a high

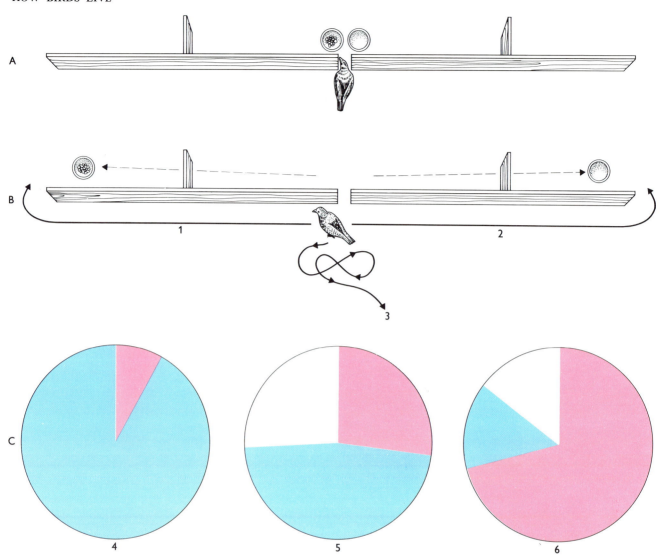

An experiment to show how birds differ in their ability to learn. In (A), a bird is presented with two dishes, only one of which contains food. It sees the dishes through a slot and immediately turns to the dish that contains food. In (B), the dishes are separated and the bird has three choices: it can move to the left to find the food (1); it can move to the right (2); and it can move in a random manner (3). The results of this experiment are shown in (C), in which correct moves (1) are represented by red, moves to the right (2) are represented by white, and random movements (3) by blue. Pigeons had the lowest rate of success (4), hens were reasonably successful (5), while crows, magpies and ravens (6) were most likely to succeed.

level and could even be construed as showing a conscience! It also showed that the jackdaw had remembered the positions of the baits in the first three boxes and that it 'counted mentally' as it bowed.

Apparently this jackdaw never behaved in the same way again. It was an isolated instance of remarkable behaviour and we must count ourselves lucky that it was performed in front of a competent observer under controlled conditions. If it had been observed casually, there would have been a good chance that little significance or even credulity would have been attached to it. This is a drawback

to answering the question of what heights of intelligence animals can show rather than the general level of intelligence they show in their everyday lives. The same applies to humans: we are all capable of flashes of inspiration beyond our normal mental capacity. From the strictly functional point of view it is an animal's or a species' normal behaviour and intelligence that are important, but the flash of genius of a Green heron or a jackdaw catch our imagination. Such flashes are rare and are usually limited to anecdotal accounts which, by their nature, are difficult to assess. From time to time there appear descriptions of birds showing an unusual degree of care for their offspring. Tits have been seen coaxing their young into the air for the first time and there are stories of birds rescuing newly fledged young that have landed on the ground and have been unable to take-off. If these stories are accurate, it means that birds are sometimes capable of appreciating an unusual situation and deciding on an appropriate and often novel course of action.

Flocks of Birds. In the study of animal and human behaviour it is becoming the practice to study groups of individuals and their interactions rather than to study an isolated individual. In a later chapter the functions of gregariousness during the breeding season will be discussed, but many birds are also gregarious outside the breeding season and may form flocks after nesting solitarily. We take it so much for granted that birds live in flocks that special names have been coined for particular species, but the very word 'flock' suggests a formless, huddled 'clump' of birds. It is now being realized that flocks of birds, herds of antelope and

schools of fishes have definite structures which are related to their function. Furthermore, birds do not fly around in flocks just for the company; flocking confers considerable advantages.

The study of an individual allows analysis of components of behaviour and gives insight into the workings of the brain, but by studying animals in groups we are learning more about their natural way of life, because most animals live in societies rather than as individuals. As an example, one can imagine that a study of single chaffinches foraging will yield information on their food preferences and the manner in which they search out and pick up their food. This is valuable information but it gives an incomplete picture because chaffinches often forage in flocks during the winter.

Flocks of tits and finches form in late summer when young birds leave their parents and band together. Later, the parents give up their territories and join the flocks. The advantages of these flocks are twofold but are based on a single concept: several pairs of eyes are better than one. This means

A mixed flock of knot *Calidris canutus* and dunlin *Calidris alpina.* In the winter both species congregate around European shores in vast flocks. The birds feed together on mudbanks and, when airborne, they fly in dense clouds that wheel and swoop in unison.

A Long-eared owl *Asio otus* in a threat posture. It fluffs out its feathers and spreads its feathers so that it appears twice its usual size. Combined with the staring eyes, hissing and a loud snapping of the bill, the display is effective in driving intruders away from the nest. It is the sudden, 'explosive' appearance of the owl that frightens the intruder. Many owls perform this display and it appears to be instinctive as young owls in the nest will perform when disturbed.

that, on one hand, the birds can find a source of food more readily and, on the other, they are less likely to be suprised by a predator.

A flock of small birds travelling through a wood exploits the food available much more efficiently than the same number of birds feeding individually. With several working together, one will soon come across an item of food. The others will quickly gather in the same spot, like vultures gathering at a carcase from many miles apart. They also note what has been found and start looking for the same sort of food in the same sort of place. While this food lasts the birds feed rapidly but as it gets used up they start to move on, peering about until a new source of food is found.

As the birds feed, be they finches, tits or pigeons,

they have to be constantly on the watch for predators that swoop without warning from the sky or lurk in ambush. Watching a tit feeding by itself at a bird table gives a very good idea of what it means for a small bird to be on the alert. Between each peck at the food, the tit swings its head about so that it can scan the landscape in all directions. With several pairs of eyes on the alert, the chances a predator making a surprise attack are reduced and it is probable that each bird can relax its vigilance and spend more time feeding. It has been found that solitary Wood pigeons spend more time looking around and less time feeding than do the members of a flock.

Among those birds which have well organized flocks there are mechanisms for thwarting the

that, through accident or weakness, has become separated from the rest.

As not all birds live in flocks, even for part of the year, they must have some particular reason for avoiding the benefits of a communal life. Birds of prey will only be seen in parties when on migration or if there is an overwhelming abundance of food. Normally, when they have to search for well hidden or wary animals they will have a greater chance of success by hunting alone. Flocking behaviour becomes advantageous when food is concentrated in large clumps. Thus flocking is found particularly among seabirds that feed on shoals of fish, and land birds that feed on seeds and fruit. Among seabirds, 'rafts' of cormorants and shags can be seen swimming slowly forward. At intervals, individuals put their heads below water to look for fish. If fish are sighted, the cormorant dives, closely followed by its companions. The cormorants benefit from charging at a shoal of fish like a squadron of cavalry because if a fish escapes one cormorant by jinking, it may fall foul of another.

The biggest, non-breeding flocks are found among the fruit and seed-eaters. These birds have to exploit foods that are locally abundant for restricted periods of time. It is advantageous for a crowd to descend on a crop of fruit or seeds at one time, strip it and move on. Because man grows his food in the form of large crops of fruits and seeds these birds become important pests.

The budgerigar is a small parrot, one of many species living in Australia. It is famous over the world as a gaudy, talkative cage bird but in Australia it is a pest. The original food of the budgerigar was composed mainly of seeds of wild grasses so it it is not surprising that they soon took to feeding on grain crops when Australia was opened to agriculture. Budgerigars live in the drier parts of Australia and survive periods of drought by moving about in flocks of tens of thousands in search of food and water. The cockatoos of Australia are close relatives of the budgerigar, but most of them prefer more wooded country. However, they too form nomadic flocks that roam the country in search of food. It seems that their defence against predators is well organized. It is said that one cockatoo keeps guard in a tree while the rest feed on the ground. When it has done its fair share, it flies down and pecks another cockatoo, who takes over the watch.

Individual Distance and Peck Order. One behavioural faculty is essential if a bird is to join a flock. It must tolerate the proximity of its fellows.

attacks of predators. The appearance of a predator sends the birds flying up in a tight bunch, perhaps in response to an alarm call. At first sight a tightly packed flock of birds might seem an easy target for a predator. If a falcon dived blindly into a flock of starlings or waders, it ought to catch something, but the opposite is found to be true. The tight formation acts as a deterrent because the confusing effect of a mass of moving birds. Consider a tennis player who accidentally drops one ball. He catches it easily as it bounces. But if he drops a box of tennis balls he is unlikely to catch any unless, by an effort of will, he avoids the distraction of several balls bouncing around him and concentrates on one. The best chance a predator has of securing a meal from a flock of birds is by pouncing on one

When watching birds feeding together, as at a bird table, it is apparent that they tolerate each other's company only to a certain extent and there are constant squabbles as individuals come too close to each other. The limit of tolerance is called the individual distance and can be measured by watching interactions between birds. The individual distance of a species varies according to the situation. During the breeding season a male songbird will not tolerate another bird near him, except for his mate, with whom, by the process of courtship, he has reduced the individual distance to zero. Outside the breeding season, the songbird may develop a tolerance for others and join a flock.

The tolerance of one bird for others in its flock is variable because the flock is a hierarchy rather than a commune. Some birds are dominant over others and there may be a rigid order of dominance in small flocks when individuals recognize each other. This is exemplified by the barnyard chicken where the order of dominance is called the peck order. The superior bird, A, can peck all the other chickens. She has first choice of food, chooses the best roosting place and is first through the henhouse door. The next in line, B, can peck everyone except A and is second in precedence for all activities. C can peck everyone except A and B. D cannot peck A, B or C and so on, until we reach the poor unfortunate at the bottom of the peck order who is pecked by everyone and cannot retaliate. She is literally henpecked. The peck order is decided by fighting but, once established, it is maintained without violence. Each bird knows its place in society and only an occasional peck is needed as a reminder if it forgets itself. This is of great advantage to the birds, as the majority can spend more time feeding without interruption. Only those at the bottom of the peck order suffer, and they suffer for the greater good of the community. In flocks of mixed sexes, like those of jackdaws, the peck order becomes more complicated. Jackdaws mate for life and a subordinate female assumes the social position of her higher-ranking mate. On the other hand, a female jackdaw will never marry beneath herself.

Communal Roosting. The individual distance between flocking birds is usually sufficient to prevent too much conflict when feeding. Individual distance also keeps individuals apart in communal roosts and allows each bird to settle itself, preen and take-off without interfering with its neighbours.

Communal roosting is seen mainly in those birds which feed in flocks. To most people, starlings are the most sensational example of birds that roost communally. As night falls they can be seen streaming into city centres and taking up position along the ledges of buildings and on trees in parks. Roosts may contain millions of birds and branches break under their weight. Queleas also roost by the million and many other birds, from blackbirds and Cattle egrets to gulls and ducks, form lesser roosts. A recent suggestion as to the value of communal roosting is that the roosts act as a centre where information concerning sources of food can be distributed. It seems that when the roost disperses in the morning groups of birds that fed badly on the previous day join those that fed well and follow them to their feeding ground.

Individual distance may be reduced to zero during roosting. Parties of Long-tailed tits, wrens, barbets and treecreepers are known to cluster in a roosting hollow so that they look like large fluffy balls. Throughout most of America, from the southern U.S.A. to Argentina, there live the anis, members of the cuckoo family which live in flocks. The anis are remarkably sociable because several pairs defend a joint territory and the females lay their eggs in a communal nest. Incubation and the feeding of the young is shared. Anis roost at night on the branches of trees. Each flock huddles together, with feathers fluffed out to keep each other warm. This is strange behaviour for a bird of warm climates but temperature measurements on two Smooth-billed anis suggest that they get chilled easily. During the day the anis' body temperature was 41°C but it dropped during the night to 33°–34°C.

It is less surprising to find that Emperor penguins huddle together for warmth. Emperor penguins lay their eggs in the total darkness of the Antarctic winter. Each carries its egg balanced on its feet so that it can shuffle about. When the weather is at its most severe, with the temperature dropping to −80°C, the penguins gather in large, tightly packed, groups that sometimes number several thousands. Each penguin rests its bill on the shoulder of the bird in front and presses close to it. Penguins on the outside of the huddle continually try to force

Skimmers are gregarious throughout the year. During the ▷ breeding season they collect in noisy flocks on exposed sand-bars which occur in river beds in the tropics during the hot dry season. In such localities nesting takes place. The nests are unlined scoops made by the birds crouching and rotating their bodies in the sand.

Blue tits *Parus caeruleus* feed at a bird table. Several birds gather to feed together but they do not move too close to one another. If another tit lands in the group it will be either driven away or one of those already in position will be displaced. The tolerance that birds show for their fellows is measured as the individual distance, the smallest distance that they can approach one another without friction. The individual distance varies according to the situation. Where food is plentiful, the tits become more tolerant and there is the advantage that they can co-operate in watching for predators.

their way into the centre, so that all get a chance to benefit. When protected by their neighbours from the weather, Emperor penguins can reduce their heat loss by one sixth. This is an important saving, because their food reserves have to last for the six weeks of incubation.

Senses

The control of flight, particularly at take-off and landing or when using air currents to soar, requires a very sensitive sensory system. To keep its balance during flight, a bird must have detailed knowledge of the positions of the wings and tail and of the tensions within the muscles controling them. It must also have rapid reactions. As it comes in to land on a perch, altering its posture, braking with its wings and extending its legs to touch down at a precise point, it must have perfect control over its muscles. It also has to know exactly where it is at any moment, the distance to the perch and the position of obstacles, must be judged to the exact fraction. So, from their beginnings in the trees where they leapt and glided from branch to branch, birds needed a fast acting sensory system that gives details in three dimensions. This led to a major difference in the sensory systems of birds and mammals.

The early mammals lived on the ground and may have been mainly nocturnal. They developed the sense of smell as prey or predators leave a scent trail on the ground that can be detected or followed for a considerable time. Scent marks are also used to mark territories or to signal information on sex and reproductive state. The sense of smell is of little use to birds, as odours sink to the ground and are dispersed by the wind so that they cannot give precise directional information. So the primitive birds came to depend on vision rather than a sense of smell. Visual information reaches the eyes at the speed of light and immense quantities of information are available because all objects are visible during the day and, to a lesser extent, by night as

The Tawny owl *Strix aluco* hunts at night for small animals by means of acute vision and hearing. Its sight is 35-100 times more sensitive than ours and it can hear sounds 10 times fainter than we can.

The ears of birds are usually covered by feathers but they are exposed on the near naked head of the ostrich. There is no external pinna as in mammals, and the meatus, the tube leading into the ear, is short. In the ostrich the meatus is so short that the eardrum is clearly visible.

well. On the other hand, few objects give off sound and it is consequently not surprising to find that those mammals that also evolved a tree-dwelling, leaping, way of life, that is, the primates and the squirrels, also have good vision.

Keen Vision. The eye of a bird is basically the same as in man but is proportionately larger and more sensitive. Some eagles have eyes larger than those of a man. The large size increases the number of light-sensitive cells that can be packed into the layer of cells at the back of the eye called the retina. The number and density of these cells determine the sensitivity, or acuity, of the eye. Small birds have small eyes and therefore relatively few retinal cells but these are packed very tightly and their visual acuity, the smallest angle that the eye can resolve, can be as little as one third of a minute of arc, half that resolved by the human eye, so their eyesight may be twice as good as ours. The record for visual acuity is probably held by the European buzzard in which there is a maximum density of one million retinal cells per mm^2. In the human eye the maximum density is 125,000 per mm^2, making the buzzard's visual acuity eight times better than ours. The area where the retinal cells are densest is known as the fovea and is so placed on the retina that it receives light from the object at which the eye is directed. In other words, when we look closely at an object, its image falls directly on the ultra-sensitive fovea. The eyes of mammals and many birds have one fovea each but some birds, particularly those that feed on the wing, have two,

and sometimes three, foveae. In these cases one fovea is so placed that it receives light from objects to the side of the head while the others are used in binocular vision. They are situated at the back of the eyeball and receive light coming from objects just in front of the head.

The eye of a bird has two structures which are found in the reptilian eye but not in that of mammals. The pecten is a comb-like structure that sticks out from the retina. It is well supplied with blood vessels and is thought to be a means of supplying food to the rest of the eye, which lacks blood vessels. The other structure is the nictitating membrane, or 'third eyelid', which acts as a sort of windscreen wiper. The proper eyelids are closed only during sleep and birds blink with the nictitating membrane. It is pulled across the exposed part of the eyeball to remove dirt, the underside being provided with microscopic brush-like processes to sweep up particles and spread tears. The membrane is transparent so that vision is not impaired even for a moment. Diving birds use their nictitating membranes as contact lenses to correct the loss of focussing power when the eye is in contact with water. It has also been suggested that all birds close their nictitating membranes when flying, to act as goggles keeping out the cold airstream. This idea is difficult to prove because of the problem of trying to observe a transparent membrane on a moving bird.

To obtain the three dimensional vision needed to rapidly judge distances, the fields of vision of both eyes have to overlap. Each eye sees a slightly different picture and, when compared in the brain, the two pictures fuse into a single stereoscopic image. A similar process is employed in stereoscopes and three dimensional cinema films. The amount of overlapping, or binocular, vision varies between birds and is related to their way of life. Hunters have a large area of overlap, that is they have good three dimensional vision, for they need to be able to judge very precisely the position of prey. Their eyes are directed forwards and, like us, they can only see the area in front of them. Owls have a visual field of 110°, of which 70° are shared by both eyes and so are covered by binocular vision. In man, the visual field is 180° and the binocular field 140°. By contrast, ground feeding birds, which have cause to fear the hunters, have their eyes placed at the sides of their heads so that they have extremely wide visual fields but little binocular overlap. They get an all round view to warn them of the

the characteristic habit of head-bobbing. As they raise and lower their heads, objects move relative to the horizon and their distance can be estimated, for objects close to the bird will appear to move more than those that are more distant. Similar behaviour is seen in the nodding movements of chickens, pigeons and wagtails as they walk, the head-weaving of penguins and, surprisingly, the bobbing movements of owls, which already have very good binocular vision for judging distances.

Acuteness of vision goes hand-in-hand with the ability to perceive colours. The light-sensitive cells in the retina are of two kinds: rods and cones. The rods are sensitive to dim light but do not register great detail. The cones are not sensitive to dim light but in bright light allow fine detail to be seen. The cones are also responsible for colour vision. All birds that feed during the day, and some owls, have colour vision, which is also most common among those mammals that live in trees, the link between acute vision and colour vision again being emphasized. Sensitivity to colour is heightened by the presence of a coloured droplet of oil in the tip of each cone cell. The droplets are red, orange and yellow and absorb light other than red, orange and yellow respectively, so increasing the eye's sensi-

A White-faced scops owl *Otus leucotis* of Africa (above) and an Oriental hawk owl *Ninox scutulata* of eastern and southern Asia. In both, the eyes are placed in the front of the head, as in man, so that the field of view of the two eyes overlap and give the owl good three dimensional vision for judging distances. At night the pupils enlarge to allow as much light as possible into the eye where it stimulates the very sensitive retina. Owls can approach motionless prey in light intensities a thousand times darker than on a moonless, overcast night. During the day the pupils contract to cut down the light entering the eye and so avoid dazzling.

approach of a predator but do not need to judge the position of food items with any accuracy. The woodcock has eyes set high in the head and has a visual field of 360°. It can see all round and has some binocular vision to the rear as well as to the front. The bittern has eyes set low in the head, which is an advantage when searching for food just in front of its feet. When alarmed, it points its bill at the sky so that its eyes are directed forwards under its chin, giving it binocular vision and a good chance of locating the source of disturbance. Some birds of prey can also do this.

As an alternative to binocular vision, birds can judge distance by parallax, the movement of two objects relative to each other. Some waders have

tivity to these colours. The droplets also act as anti-glare filters. Glare off water is mainly of blue light which has a short wavelength and is held back by the droplets while longer wavelengths such as red, orange and yellow pass through to stimulate the cone.

Colour vision is poorest among the birds that fly at night or in dim light, but they are compensated by an extreme sensitivity to dim light. The retina of their eyes contain large numbers of red cells and their cones contain colourless oil droplets which allow all wavelengths of light to pass through, glare not being a matter of concern for them. Owls have large, tubular eyeballs with a wide cornea and lens that admit as much light as possible and the retina is packed with the highly sensitive rod cells. Owls can find motionless prey 6 ft (2 m) away in an illumination of 0.000,000,73 foot candles, a light 100 times less than that required by man.

The extreme sensitivity of birds' vision is employed in navigation during migration and homing. In a current theory of celestial navigation, described in Chapter 12, it is proposed that birds can detect the movement of the sun across the sky, a feat equivalent to seeing the movement of the hour hand of a watch. Experiments with pigeons show that this is well within their capabilities. Vision is further involved in the timing of migration and the rhythm of the breeding cycle. Daylength is an important trigger for migration, singing and, to some extent, for laying. Birds must keep an accurate, if unconscious, note of the times of sunrise and sunset and artificial lengthening of the day by street-lighting leads birds to sing unusually early in the year and to continue singing long after sunset. The Japanese art of *Yogai* consists of making cage birds sing during the winter by lengthening their days with candlelight.

Acute Hearing. Although second to vision, hearing plays an important part in the lives of birds. Songs and calls are used for communication in territorial behaviour, for giving warning of predators and for communication between mates and offspring. The sense of hearing is occasionally used for finding food particularly by owls, and perhaps by waders that may be able to hear earthworms burrowing. A select few use echo-location as a means of navigation. Most birds are sensitive to a narrower range of frequencies than are humans but they can discriminate sounds that are too rapid for the human ear to resolve. The whip-poor-will, an American nightjar, is named after its three-part song which, if recorded and played back slowly, turns out to be 'whip-*pup*-poor-will'. The human ear cannot distinguish the second syllable.

Hearing has the advantage over vision that sound waves can go round corners, while light waves move only in straight lines. As a result, birds which lead a rather furtive life in the cover of woodland generally sing well, whereas birds with gaudy plumage flaunt it from exposed perches and display grounds and have weak songs. The same properties make sounds very useful for alarm signals. They can be uttered from cover and can be received by other birds whose attention is directed elsewhere. A characteristic of many alarm calls warning of a predator's presence is that it is difficult to tell what direction they come from, so protecting the alarm-raiser. When a chaffinch sees a hawk overhead it rushes for cover and gives a single 'seet' call. It is only delivered once and its physical characteristics make it difficult for the hawk to detect the chaffinch's perch, but other chaffinches are alerted and also make for safety. On the other hand, if the hawk or an owl is perching conspicuously, chaffinches, and other small birds, gather round to mob it. They make no attempt to hide themselves and will even fly after it. They utter repeated 'chink' calls whose repetition and low pitch make them easy to locate and so draw other birds' attention to the position of the predator.

Hearing becomes increasingly important in the absence of light. Most birds become inactive at night and leave the air to the bats. The few birds that are abroad by night have extremely good vision. As mentioned earlier, owls have extremely good vision in poor light, which is essential for flying through dimly lit woods, but for finding their prey, they rely mainly on hearing. A large eardrum and other refinements of structure make an owl's hearing extremely acute and its ability to judge the direction of a sound is enhanced by the asymmetric placing of the ears on the head and by a small flap of skin that directs sound into the ear, like the pinnae, or ear flaps, of mammals. The efficacy of

The bittern *Botaurus stellaris* on its nest among the reeds. ▷ Bitterns are shy and difficult to find in dense reed beds. During the breeding season their presence is given away by the deep booming calls of the male. Their concealment is enhanced by their habit of standing with the bill pointing skywards when alarmed. The dark vertical stripes on the neck blend in with the reeds and, if there is a wind, the bittern sways with the reeds. At the same time the bittern is able to get a good view of the disturbance by turning its eyes to look under its chin.

Taking Advantage of Plenty

The high metabolic rate and the energy requirements for flight make an efficient digestive system essential for birds. The breakdown and absorption of food leaves little waste and birds produce very small amounts of droppings. Digestion is also very rapid; berries can pass through a thrush in 30 minutes. But apart from being faster and more efficient, the alimentary system of birds is essentially similar to that of mammals except at the start of the digestive process. The main difference is that birds have no teeth. Food is manipulated by the bill and is usually swallowed whole. At the most it is broken into smaller pieces, as in flesh-tearing and seed-cracking species. Mammals chew their food and mix it with a saliva that contains digestive enzymes. By contrast, birds break up their food in a two-chambered stomach. The anterior chamber, called the proventriculus, secretes enzymes and hydrochloric acid which start to break down the food. The acid is often strong enough to dissolve bones. The posterior chamber, the gizzard, has a strong muscular wall which contracts rhythmically to knead the food. Many birds, from ostriches to the domestic chicken, swallow grit to help the kneading process and the 18th-century Italian biologist Spallanzani found that a turkey could grind up 12 steel needles in 36 hours.

Colonization by the birds of a wide variety of habitats has been made possible to a large extent by their exploitation of a great range of foods. They have evolved different shapes of bill, and different food searching habits, either towards specialization for a particular food or towards a more liberal diet.

The Advantages of Bolting Food. By gulping their food with little treatment, birds can take in large quantities in a short time. Overloading of the digestive system is prevented by storage. Fish eaters store food in the proventriculus and members of the crow family carry food in a throat pouch, but the majority of birds store food in the crop, a thin-walled bag that leads off the throat. When a bird is replete the distended crop shows as a distinct bulge in the neck. A bird benefits in several ways from being able to assimilate large amounts of food in a short time. Securing a large meal in a short

Four species of tit live together in European woodland. They are, from the left, Coal tit *Parus ater*, Blue tit *P. caeruleus*, Great tit *P. major* and Marsh tit *P. palustris*. Although they all have the same diet of insects, they do not compete for food. Each species feeds in a slightly different place. For instance, on a single tree Blue tits forage on the smaller twigs while Marsh tits feed on bigger boughs.

time allows a bird to satisfy its hunger and make the most of a source of food before its fellows arrive to compete. In the Antarctic, a dead seal attracts hordes of Giant petrels, goose-sized relatives of the albatrosses. These birds are the vultures of the south. They push their heads deep into the seal carcase, getting their feathers smothered in blood, and gorge themselves until they can take no more. To get a full meal a Giant petrel has to compete with its fellows and lengthy battles may take place, but when full, it can amble away and rest by the shore to digest its meal in peace. The drawback comes when the Giant petrels are disturbed at their meal and must seek the safety of the air. Those that have not fed, run over the sea, flapping their wings until they soar away safely, but the gorged birds are too heavy and are unable to take-off. To get airborne they have to cast out ballast by regurgitating their hard-won meal. A big meal may be a hindrance to a Giant petrel when faced by an enemy, but for many birds the ability to store food is a definite advantage because it reduces the time needed to feed. The time spent on the ground, searching for seeds or insects is a

these arrangements was shown by a Barn owl that could pounce accurately on a mouse or a ball of paper dragged behind a length of string, in a completely lightproof room.

Two, perhaps three, birds have developed systems of echo-location for finding their way in the dark. The oilbird of northern South America, a relative of the nightjars, feeds at night on the oily fruits of palm trees. It uses its good eyesight while feeding but it nests in pitch dark caves where vision is impossible. The nests are on ledges on the cave walls and are located by the returning oilbirds by echo-location. They emit a continuous stream of clicks, which can be heard by the human ear, and determine the position of the nests by the echoes bouncing off the cave walls. The Cave swiftlets of south-east Asia also use echo-location to find their way about caves. The exception is one species of swiftlet that lives at the cave entrance where there is sufficient light to see its nest. It is also possible that some penguins find fish by echo-location. Tests have been carried out in a special echo-free tank. Fish were thrown into the tank, and as the penguins dived in, the lights were turned off, leaving total darkness. Within 30 seconds all the fish had been eaten. The penguins were not using their voices to produce the necessary train of sounds but were probably using sounds of the turbulance caused by the beating of their flippers.

Weak Smell. By contrast to sight and hearing, a bird's senses of smell, touch and taste are poor. Sensitivity to pressure, or touch, may be important in detecting changes in airflow over the body during flight and when probing for food in earth or rotten wood, but for the recognition of food, sight is the most important sense. If an object looks edible, a bird eats it, placing little reliance on taste or smell, although birds of prey reject rotten meat. It is thought that the petrel family, the vultures and the oilbird of Trinidad may have a better sense of smell than most birds. Experiments in the laboratory have shown that several birds are sensitive to odours but what use they make of a sense of smell is not known. There are few observations of the sense of smell being used in the wild. The honeyguides of Africa are attracted by the smell of burning bees' wax and petrels are attracted to hot fat poured on the sea. Turkey vultures have been attracted to the fumes of foul smelling ethyl mercaptan which were carried aloft in thermals. The vultures followed the fumes down to the bottom of a canyon where the mercaptan had been released.

The kiwi is the one bird that is known to use its

The woodcock *Scolopax rusticola* nests throughout Europe and northern Asia. Its grey-brown and rufous plumage make it almost impossible to see as it sits among low herbage. But the woodcock is well aware of what is taking place around it. Its eyes are on the sides of its head and are protuberant, giving it a 360° field of vision. The fields of vision of each eye overlap both in front and behind the head so that the woodcock has three dimensional vision to the front and rear. Woodcock feed by probing the soil for worms and insects. They can probably peer along the bill to see their prey and, at the same time, keep a lookout in all directions for enemies.

Oilbird *Steatornis caripensis* on its nest in a South American cave. Oilbirds leave their nests at night to feed on fruit, particularly the oily fruit of palms. They have good vision and an unusually well-developed sense of smell which may be used for finding the fruit. Oilbirds are also one of the few birds to use echolocation. They emit a continuous stream of audible clicks and use the echoes to find the position of their nest ledges in the pitch dark caves.

sense of smell for finding food. It finds earthworms by probing with its bill, as do many waders, but waders are using touch or even peering down the hole made by the bill. Kiwis have the nostrils placed in a unique position at the tip of the bill, and experiments have shown that they can detect worms buried in aluminium tubes by scent alone. A series of tubes covered with fine nylon netting were sunk in the ground and the kiwis learnt to search for them. When some were baited and others left empty only the coverings of those containing bait were pierced by the kiwis.

Taking Advantage of Plenty

The high metabolic rate and the energy requirements for flight make an efficient digestive system essential for birds. The breakdown and absorption of food leaves little waste and birds produce very small amounts of droppings. Digestion is also very rapid; berries can pass through a thrush in 30 minutes. But apart from being faster and more efficient, the alimentary system of birds is essentially similar to that of mammals except at the start of the digestive process. The main difference is that birds have no teeth. Food is manipulated by the bill and is usually swallowed whole. At the most it is broken into smaller pieces, as in flesh-tearing and seed-cracking species. Mammals chew their food and mix it with a saliva that contains digestive enzymes. By contrast, birds break up their food in a two-chambered stomach. The anterior chamber, called the proventriculus, secretes enzymes and hydrochloric acid which start to break down the food. The acid is often strong enough to dissolve bones. The posterior chamber, the gizzard, has a strong muscular wall which contracts rhythmically to knead the food. Many birds, from ostriches to the domestic chicken, swallow grit to help the kneading process and the 18th-century Italian biologist Spallanzani found that a turkey could grind up 12 steel needles in 36 hours.

Colonization by the birds of a wide variety of habitats has been made possible to a large extent by their exploitation of a great range of foods. They have evolved different shapes of bill, and different food searching habits, either towards specialization for a particular food or towards a more liberal diet.

The Advantages of Bolting Food. By gulping their food with little treatment, birds can take in large quantities in a short time. Overloading of the digestive system is prevented by storage. Fish eaters store food in the proventriculus and members of the crow family carry food in a throat pouch, but the majority of birds store food in the crop, a thin-walled bag that leads off the throat. When a bird is replete the distended crop shows as a distinct bulge in the neck. A bird benefits in several ways from being able to assimilate large amounts of food in a short time. Securing a large meal in a short

Four species of tit live together in European woodland. They are, from the left, Coal tit *Parus ater*, Blue tit *P. caeruleus*, Great tit *P. major* and Marsh tit *P. palustris*. Although they all have the same diet of insects, they do not compete for food. Each species feeds in a slightly different place. For instance, on a single tree Blue tits forage on the smaller twigs while Marsh tits feed on bigger boughs.

time allows a bird to satisfy its hunger and make the most of a source of food before its fellows arrive to compete. In the Antarctic, a dead seal attracts hordes of Giant petrels, goose-sized relatives of the albatrosses. These birds are the vultures of the south. They push their heads deep into the seal carcase, getting their feathers smothered in blood, and gorge themselves until they can take no more. To get a full meal a Giant petrel has to compete with its fellows and lengthy battles may take place, but when full, it can amble away and rest by the shore to digest its meal in peace. The drawback comes when the Giant petrels are disturbed at their meal and must seek the safety of the air. Those that have not fed, run over the sea, flapping their wings until they soar away safely, but the gorged birds are too heavy and are unable to take-off. To get airborne they have to cast out ballast by regurgitating their hard-won meal. A big meal may be a hindrance to a Giant petrel when faced by an enemy, but for many birds the ability to store food is a definite advantage because it reduces the time needed to feed. The time spent on the ground, searching for seeds or insects is a

period of danger. It is an advantage to be able to stuff the crop with food and get back to the safety of the trees.

A final advantage of food-storing appears in the breeding season. Many birds have to collect food for their young. This is a full time job and may involve considerable journeys, especially in desert-living or oceanic birds. The pure white Snow petrel and the brown and white Antarctic petrel achieve what are probably the record feeding flights. These petrels usually nest on cliffs overlooking the sea but colonies have been found in the Theron mountains, 150 miles deep into the Antarctic mainland. To get food for their nestlings the adult petrels have to make a round trip overland of at least 300 miles, often in extremely bad weather. When they reach the coast, their journey is not over because they have to fly over the frozen sea to find open water where they can fish.

Bills of Many Shapes. Birds collect their food by adroit use of the bill, an organ whose primary function is to pick up food and only secondarily to build nests or to preen feathers. The shape of the bill is adapted to the nature of the food and the means

by which it is obtained, so it is a good indicator of the kind of food a bird eats and of its feeding habits. A few examples will illustrate this. Swifts and nightjars have short weak bills with a very wide gape surrounded by a palisade of bristles. These birds feed on flying insects and the widely opened mouth and surrounding bristles form a scoop for collecting insects at speed. The waders typically have long, slender bills, often curved, and they use them for probing sand or earth for small animals. The kiwi also has a long bill which it uses for finding earthworms. The lower half of the skimmer's bill is longer than the upper half. It flies low over the sea, trailing the lower half in the water as a scoop to pick up fish.

A complete catalogue of bill shapes is a lengthy one; there are the tough seed-crackers of the parrots, the tearing hooks of owls and hawks, the stabbing spears of the herons and many others but no list is complete without mention of the extinct New Zealand huia. It is unfortunate that the huia became extinct around 1910, before it had been studied properly. It is the only bird in which the two sexes had radically different bills. The males

The Common crossbill *Loxia curvirostris* showing the crossed tips of the bill. This is an adaptation for removing the seeds from conifer cones. Crossbills eat little other than conifer seeds. A crop of seeds stays in the cones almost the whole year. Only for a few weeks, between the cones ripening and dropping their seeds and the new crop forming, do crossbills turn to insects and other seeds for food.

Sheathbills *Chionis alba* are the only birds living in the Antarctic that do not have webbed feet. They look like white pigeons and are named after the horny sheath covering the base of the bill. Sheathbills eat algae, limpets and other shore animals but they are also scavengers. They eat dead seals, the placentas of seals and even pick at the wounds of live seals. During the summer they take penguin eggs and they feed their chicks on krill stolen from penguins.

of some hornbills have larger and more elaborate bills than the females as a sexual adornment, but the bills of the male and female huia reflect different feeding habits. The male's bill was strong and chisel-shaped, like that of a woodpecker, while the female's was slender and down-curved. In many books it is stated that a pair of huias would co-operate in feeding. The male is supposed to have chiselled grubs out of decayed wood with its straight bill and the female probed for grubs in rougher wood with her slender pliable bill. Occasionally, so the story goes, the male would be unable to extract the grub with its short bill and the female would come to its aid. It has even been suggested that such help was indispensable and that the pair formed a functional unit when feeding. If this was true, it would be very remarkable and one wonders how young, unmated huias survived on their own. The fact of the matter is that our knowledge of the huia's habits comes from an account by Sir Walter Buller who kept a pair in an aviary in 1864. His description is rather ambiguously worded. After describing the manner in which his huias picked out grubs from a log, Buller recounted how the male huia was sometimes unable to reach a grub after it had been exposed. Then the female would 'at once come to his aid' and pick the grub out with her long bill. The choice of phrase was bad; the female did not 'come to his aid', nor were the insects for them 'both to enjoy'. She ate the grub herself. There was no more co-operation between the huias than there is between a group of gulls, sparrows, crows or vultures. It was every man for himself. Nevertheless, that the two sexes should have different feeding habits is still remarkable and it must remain a matter of regret that the huia is extinct, so that we shall never know exactly what they did.

Co-operative Feeding. Co-operation in feeding is a feature in the behaviour of many species of birds but the advantage lies in the finding of food rather than in its exploitation. Flocks of tits searching in trees for tiny insects and seeds feed more efficiently than single birds because a number of birds have a better chance of finding a given item of food than does a single bird on its own. Once a member of the flock has found an item of food, the remainder of the flock start to search for similar items in the same sort of place.

A deliberate form of co-operative feeding is seen

in the strange story of the honeyguide and Honey badgers. The honeyguides are small birds that live in Africa and Southern Asia. They would be of interest for their cuckoo-like breeding habits alone but they are best known for the way two of the 12 species co-operate with Honey badgers and even men to raid nests of wild bees. The Black-throated and Scaly-throated honeyguides have developed a well marked habit of drawing the attention of a badger or man to a bees' nest by repeatedly calling and displaying by fanning the tail to show off white markings. When the helper starts to follow, the honeyguide flies a short way towards the nest and settles on a perch. As the helper catches up, the bird moves on again, repeating its calls and flights until the nest is reached. While the bees' nest is being torn open, the honeyguide perches silently, content to wait for the grubs and honeycomb that are left. Africans used to make sure that some comb was left for the honeyguide and they valued the bird's assistance so much that they would imitate the growls of a Honey badger to coax the

honeyguide into leading them to a nest. Nowadays, with the standard of living rising in Africa, buying sugar is preferable to running the risk of being stung. The honeyguides appear to have learnt that men are no longer willing helpers and are giving up trying to coax them.

It was some time before it was realized that honeyguides ate the wax of the comb rather than the honey. Wax is normally very indigestible but the honeyguides have bacteria in their intestines which break it down. They are also sensitive to the smell of wax, a fact noted as long ago as 1569 when a Portuguese missionary reported that honeyguides flew into his church when he burnt beeswax candles. Recently this observation has been repeated by burning candles placed in trees; and it has also been found that honeyguides have large olfactory lobes in the brain. This, with the kiwi, is another rare example of a bird using the sense of smell.

The behaviour of the honeyguide is remarkable because it requires the active co-operation of another kind of animal. If the honeyguide were merely to follow a Honey badger and pick up the leavings of its meals, its behaviour would be nothing out of the ordinary. Plenty of birds make use of other animals to provide food for them. There are the gulls and albatrosses which follow ships for refuse thrown overboard, the European robin which waits for worms turned up by the gardener and several tropical birds, such as hornbills, which follow troops of monkeys to pick up the food they drop. Carmine bee-eaters go one step further. They feed on the insects stirred up by large birds like the Kori bustard and save energy by riding on the big birds' backs.

The value of following another animal for the food it provides has been demonstrated beyond doubt by the Cattle egret. This remarkable bird has spread from the Old World to America, where it ranges as far north as Ontario, and to Australia. It is also unusual for an egret in that it feeds on land rather than in water. Flocks of Cattle egrets feed on grassland, the birds at the rear leapfrogging over their fellows so that all get a turn in the front as the flock rolls slowly forward. The movements of the egrets disturbs insects which fly up and are caught. The flocks also follow cattle to catch the insects that they disturb and in their native Africa they follow antelopes and zebra. Nowadays they follow farm vehicles. In the heat of the day, when the cattle lie up, the egrets have to forage for themselves. But when the cattle are feeding, the egrets gather around, thereby catching one and a half times the number of insects they would catch when working

◁ Feral pigeons in Trafalgar Square, London. They are descended from domestic Rock doves *Columba livia*. The feral or 'town' pigeon is dependent on man for food and shelter. Ledges on buildings provide roosting and nesting places and food is scavenged. At one time grain spilt from horses' nosebags was an important food, now bread is the main food. Although feral pigeons are often deliberately fed, they are a major nuisance through fouling buildings and they are a potential health hazard. As their diet is often deficient they will even peck away the mortar between bricks to obtain the lime necessary for eggshells.

American greater flamingos *Phoenicopterus* ▷ *ruber* resting and preening. Their long necks and legs enable them to feed in salt lakes and lagoons. The banana-shaped bill is held upside-down and minute organisms are filtered out by sucking water through rows of hairs. Greater flamingos feed at the surface of the water and in the mud at the bottom, whereas Lesser flamingos feed only at the surface. The delicate pink coloration is caused by pigments extracted from the food. Captive flamingos are given pigment additives in their food to preserve their colours.

The shoveler *Spatula clypeata* feeds by swimming through the water and sieving water through its bill. The English and scientific names refer to the heavy spoon-shaped bill which is continually thrust into the water. The shoveler's main haunts are marshes, swamps and shallow, muddy pools where there is a fringe of vegetation. The dabbling action of the bill draws water through the comb-like lamellae which fringe the bill and filter out small aquatic animals and plants.

Griffon vultures gather around a carcase. Up to 100 may gather to feed on the flesh of a large animal. The hungriest vultures push their way to the front and gorge themselves on soft tissues until they are displaced in turn. The ability to bolt their food is a decided advantage and, once replete, the vulture moves a short distance and settles down to digest its meal.

alone, at a saving of one third of the energy expended.

Spearing Snails. The Everglade or Snail kite is one of the few birds to have a very restricted diet. It is common in swampy parts of Central and South America, but is now very rare in the Everglades of Florida. It feeds entirely on the Apple snail, a large water snail, which it catches in its talons and removes delicately from its shell. The feeding posts of Everglade kites are easily recognized by the piles of empty shells, which are quite undamaged. The method of feeding is to fly with a snail to the feeding post. The snail will have withdrawn into its shell at the first alarm, but the kite waits patiently for the snail to cautiously emerge then spears its body with the long, curved tip of its bill. The snail tries to retreat again, but the violent muscular contraction tears its body from the inner wall of the shell. The kite then shakes its head, the shell flies off, and the snail is swallowed.

This 'winkle-picking' behaviour is very neat but one wonders why the Everglade kite should go to so much trouble to get rid of the shell when other birds of prey are capable of swallowing animals whole and later regurgitating the shells and bones. It seems that evolution in this instance has been unnecessarily elaborate, although the limpkin, an odd wading bird that lives in the same habitat as the Everglade kite, also feeds on Apple snails by picking them out of their shells. The limpkin wedges a snail in a crevice, waits for it to emerge then spears the body with the curved lower half of the bill and severs the main muscle in the snail's body.

Filter Feeders. A variety of birds exploit the masses of small animals and plants that swarm near the surface of fresh and salt water by using the bill as a filter. The best known of the filter-feeding birds is the mallard. It is a familiar sight to see a mallard

dabbling in the muddy water with its bill half submerged. It sucks water into the mouth and forces it out through the sides of the bill by the action of its tongue. Along the margins of the bill, horny plates, or lamellae, act as a fine sieve or filter, holding back edible particles as the water flows past. How or, indeed, whether the mallard distinguishes edible particles from inedible rubbish is not known, except that there are rows of touch organs along the edge of the bill which suggest that it may be able to feel the difference. Many other ducks, as well as swans and geese, have lamellae in their bills and feed in the same way.

The prions, small grey relatives of the fulmar and albatrosses, form another group of filter feeders. The home of the prions is the cold waters of the Southern Ocean. They used to be called whalebirds because the plates on their bills and the way they feed by filtering out small crustaceans reminded whalers of the baleen plates and feeding habits of whales. The different species of prion are very much alike except in the appearance of the bill which is broad in some species and narrow in others. It may be that the shape of the bill is related to the precise kinds of animals that each species feeds on. This is the situation that has been found in flamingos, the filter-feeders *par excellence*. The flamingos live in salt or alkaline lakes and lagoons which are rich in microscopic plants and small animals. In the Rift Valley lakes of East Africa, where millions of flamingos cover the water in pink masses, the Greater and Lesser flamingos live side by side, but they have different feeding habits and so do not compete.

The Greater flamingo feeds by rapidly opening and closing its bill, like a duck dabbling. As the bill closes, water is squeezed out between the two mandibles and is forced through rows of stiff bristles. Small animals, such as snails, shrimps

and insect larvae are caught in the bristles and collected by the tongue. Microscopic plants are also extracted by means of fine hairs, or laminae, inside the bill. The Lesser flamingo lacks the bristles and collects only microscopic plants with the laminae. Instead of 'dabbling' it keeps its bill open and pumps water in and out by the action of its tongue. The laminae lie flat as water comes in and stand erect to intercept food as it is forced out. These differences in feeding mechanisms allow the Greater flamingo to collect food from the bottom of the lake while Lesser flamingos feed at the surface and, in calm weather, can feed while swimming at the centre of the lake.

Avoiding Competition by Specialization. There is a law in biology that similar species do not compete for food; they feed either on a slightly different type of food or take the same food at slightly different times or places. The two flamingoes on African lakes appear, at first sight, to be feeding on the same food but close examination show that both structure and behaviour lead to their having different diets. Such a subtle separation is seen among the tits living in mixed woodland. Several species may feed together in a flock but they choose slightly different places from which to gather their food. Great tits feed near the ground, Marsh tits among the shrubs up to 20 ft (6 m) above the ground and Long-tailed tits somewhat higher. Blue and Coal tits feed at all levels but competition is reduced because Blue tits prefer oaks while Coal tits prefer conifers. Even on the same trees, Blue tits stay on the smaller twigs while Marsh tits search the bigger boughs. There is some overlap of food, as there is between the two flamingos, but there is enough difference to avoid too much competition. The system is, furthermore, flexible enough for each tit to take advantage of a rich source of food. If there is a plague of caterpillars, tits of all species eat caterpillars, without competition and with plenty left over.

The finches show a more marked difference in

◁ The limpkin *Aramus guarauna* is a long-legged bird that lives in wet country from Georgia and Florida to Argentina. Its main food is the Apple snail. On finding a snail, the limpkin carries it ashore and wedges it in the fork of a tree. It waits for the snail to relax then spears the body between the shell and the horny operculum or door. A flick of the head wrenches the snail clear of its shell.

White pelicans showing their ▷ throat pouches. These are not used for carrying fish, as is often believed, but they are used as scoops for catching fish. The pelican thrusts its bill into the water and the lower mandible spreads to form a broad loop. As the head is raised, the elastic pouch sags under the weight of water trapped in it. Any fish trapped in the pouch are swallowed.

A buzzard *Buteo buteo* with a rabbit that it has caught by pouncing and seizing it in its talons.

diet, which is correlated with the shape of the bill. In general, the finches have stout, conical bills which they use for cracking seeds, but the goldfinch has a very thin bill and feeds on the soft seeds of dandelions and thistles. The linnet has a stronger bill and eats the small seeds of hemp and rape and the hawfinch has a really stout bill that allows it to crack cherry stones. The crossbill is a special case. When the young crossbill hatches, its bill has a normal shape but by the time it leaves the nest the tips of the mandibles have crossed over by growing crooked. This strange bill is used to extract the seeds from pine cones. The Parrot crossbill has a heavy bill and feeds mainly on the tough cones of pines, whereas the smaller bill of the Two-barred crossbill is used on the soft cones of larch.

The finches of the Galapagos Islands have evolved a range of bill sizes and feeding habits. They are often called Darwin's finches because they were a source of inspiration to Charles Darwin

The shape of the bird bill has been modified to take advantage of a large variety of foods. The Ground finch *Geospiza* (1) eats seeds, while the Tree finch *Camarhynchus* (2) uses a twig to probe for insects. The cockatoo (3) eats seeds and nuts, the Palaearctic crossbill *Loxia* (4) opens fir cones, and the Sicklebill humming bird (5) feeds from flowers. The Greater flamingo *Phoenicopterus* (6) has marginal hooks for filter feeding, and the Swordbill humming bird (7) feeds on flowers. The Egyptian vulture *Trigoniceps* (8) has a curved bill for tearing flesh, while a similar bill is seen in the scavenger, the Wandering albatross *Diomedea* (9). Finally, the European goosander *Mergus* (10) has a serrated bill for holding fish. The male (11) and female (12) of the extinct huia *Heterolocha acutirostris* had different bills. That of the male was used for chipping rotten wood to get at insect grubs. The female used her slender, curved bill for probing in cracks. Huias were found only in the mountain forests of North Island, New Zealand and became extinct by about 1910. It is often said that a pair of huias would co-operate in feeding, the male breaking open the wood and the female extracting the insect. There is no evidence that this remarkable behaviour occurred because the huia was extinct before the function of the sex difference in bills could be investigated. The feeding methods adopted by birds are as important as their structural adaptations. Recordings of Blue tits feeding from milk bottles in the United Kingdom during the period 1930-1935 are plotted in blue (13) and those for 1935-1947 in black. It can be seen how rapidly the new feeding method spread.

76

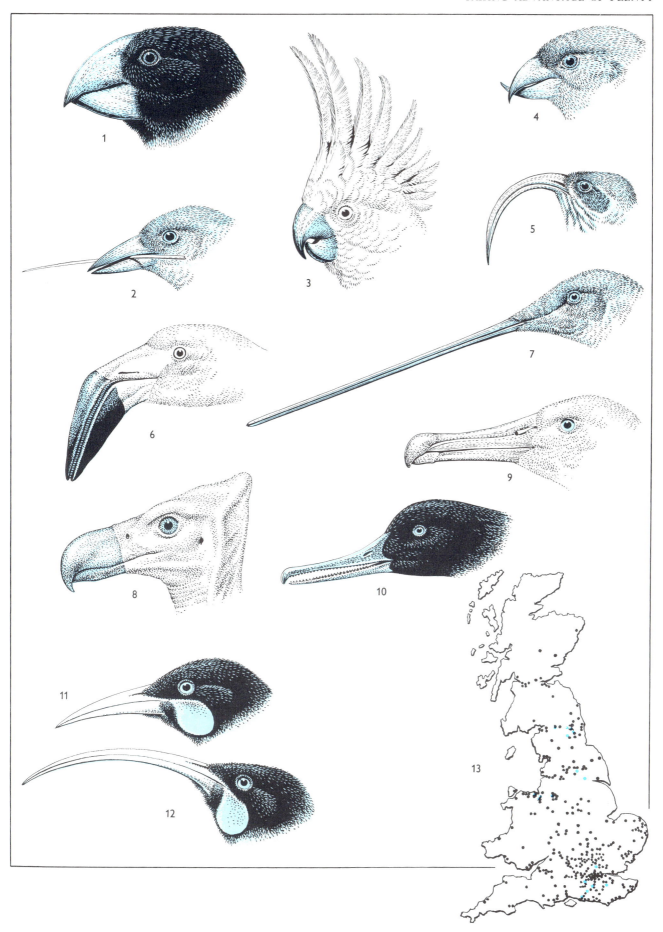

when propounding his theory of evolution by natural selection. The ancestor of these finches came to the Galapagos from the South American mainland. There were few other kinds of birds on the islands and the ancestral finch evolved into a family of 14 species which have taken advantage of the lack of competition to utilize many kinds of food. In the process they have taken up habits paralleling those of other kinds of birds. There are the Tree finches which have pointed bills and hang upside down among twigs while searching for insects, like tits. The Warbler finch also hunts for insects, sometimes catching them in the air. The parrot-like finches feed on soft fruit and the six species of Ground and Cactus finch are seed-eaters with bills that range in size from that of a chaffinch to that of a hawfinch. The most extreme of Darwin's finches are the species that feeds on small crustaceans on the seashore, another that eats gulls' eggs and has been seen to drink the blood of nesting boobies by pricking them with its sharp bill; and finally there is the famous Woodpecker finch. This behaves like a woodpecker, searching for insects hiding deep in crevices. It lacks the long tongue of the woodpeckers to extract the insects but has learnt to use cactus spines for the same purpose. The finch snaps off a cactus spine and holds it in the bill to probe crevices – one of the few instances of tool-using among birds.

Flexible Feeding Methods. While some birds have established a specialized way of life by exploiting a source of food that takes them away from competition with related species, others have developed a very liberal diet. These birds generally have an unspecialized shape of bill and are opportunists, taking advantage of periodic abundance of various foods. The European blackbird feeds mainly on plant material, particularly fruit. It will strip yew, ivy, blackberry, holly and many cultivated fruits as they come in season but it also takes many kinds of seeds, earthworms, beetles, wireworms, caterpillars, ants, snails, spiders and occasionally small fishes and frogs. Members of the crow family will also eat almost anything, including the eggs and nestlings of other birds, but the biggest opportunists are found in the gull family. They are basically fish eaters and some, like the kittiwake, eat almost nothing but fish. The Black-headed, Herring and Black-backed gulls are not so strict in their diets. They are becoming increasingly dependant on man by frequenting sewage outlets, rubbish dumps and ploughed fields, as well as following fishing boats. Herring gulls and Black-backed gulls prey on the nestlings of other birds, such as Black-headed gulls, or adult puffins and guillemots, and in some places they are persecuted for taking lambs and poultry. The American Ring-billed gull, amongst others, is noted for robbing other species of their food.

Even more of an opportunist is the Great skua, the first cousin of the gulls. The Great skua is about the size of a Herring gull but is more heavily built. It is unique among birds for breeding in both north and south temperate zones while in the southern hemisphere they also nest on the fringes of the Antarctic continent. One has even been seen flying over the South Pole. The Great skua is basically a fish eater like the gulls, but it is rare to see it fishing

The Giant petrel *Macronectes giganteus* beside its downy chick is as large as a small albatross, to which it is closely related. The main food of Giant petrels is fish, squid and krill, which is caught in the sharp-edged, hooked bill. Small seabirds are caught and Giant petrels also scavenge on land. They gather at the carcases of seals and penguins and gorge themselves on the flesh. Their bills are not strong enough to tear open the skin of a seal but they can penetrate the body orifices and thrust their heads deep inside the carcase.

The anhinga *Anhinga anhinga* is the American representative of the darter family. It ranges from southern USA to Argentina. It has a system of tendons which rapidly straightens the neck, shooting the bill forward to impale fish.

and it is most famous as a pirate, because of its spectacular habit of chasing gulls and gannets to make them disgorge their food. Its victims are birds bringing home food for their nestlings. When one is spotted, the skua gives chase, following relentlessly as the victim twists and turns to get away. It even pulls at the victim's wings and tail until the victim is harried into disgorging its load of fish, which the skua dives to catch in mid-air. The impression is often given that this is the skuas' main method of feeding, but it is a method that is used only by a few

skuas as the opportunity arises. In the southern hemisphere, skuas living on the Antarctic peninsula and in the Cape Horn region rob the Blue-eyed shag but on the Antarctic islands lying between, they leave the shags alone. On the other hand, on these islands the skuas will harry the Dominican or Southern black-backed gull. The gull hovers over a raft of shags and plunges to rob a shag of a large fish that it is having difficulty in swallowing. The gull has similar difficulties swallowing the fish and lands on the beach to tear it apart. Here the skuas are waiting, ready to confiscate the fish from the gull.

A more important source of food for Great skuas is found in the large colonies of seabirds near the skuas' own nesting grounds. In the North Atlantic, skuas are important predators of puffins and kittiwakes and, in Antarctic regions, they kill many small petrels such as prions, Storm petrels and Snow petrels. The skuas have learnt to lie in wait for the petrels as they enter or leave their burrows. Petrels are ungainly on land and the skuas pounce before they can take-off.

Penguin rookeries are also a hunting ground for skuas but the vast number of eggs and young penguins are available to the skuas only during a short period. For most of the nesting season the skuas hunt for fish, but twice during the summer they turn to the penguin rookeries for easy meals. After the penguins have laid their eggs they take a short time to settle down to incubation and, in the confusion, eggs get left unattended or kicked out of the nest. Immediately, a waiting skua pounces and carries the egg away. When incubation is under way, the skuas find little to pick up and they forage elsewhere. Their next opportunity arrives when the young penguins emerge from under their parents. The penguin chicks are small and weak and fall an easy prey to skuas if their parents are in-attentive. As the chicks grow older they become too big for the skuas to handle, and the rookeries again become unprofitable hunting grounds. Starvling's chicks abandoned by their parents, are the only food that remains for the skuas. They are harried by the skuas, who buffet and peck them until they die from exhaustion and loss of blood. Death is slow and unpleasant to watch because the skuas lack the sharp, merciful peck at the skull or the fierce squeeze of the talons used by the true hunting birds. All they can do is peck and tug with their compara-tively blunt bills until the victim succumbs.

Crops and Pests. The skua, then, is not so much a merciless pirate and murderer as a fish eater that becomes a parasite and a rather inefficient predator when opportunity allows. The true story was re-vealed only after weeks of patient work, and over the last two decades there have been many similar investigations into the relationships of birds with their food supplies. These studies have more than academic interest. Many birds are important pests of crops and, to control them efficiently and effectively, it is necessary to know the precise details of their feeding habits. Armed with this informa-tion, it is possible to suggest ways in which the birds

can be kept away from the crops or to find weak links in the birds' ecology so that they can be attacked and their numbers reduced.

The basic principle of agriculture is to shift the balance of nature in favour of a particular plant species. The aim is to have few other plants (weeds) competing with the crop and to keep away any animals that may feed on the crop. An animal becomes a pest when it upsets this artificial balance to an extent that is commercially significant. It is very easy for an animal to become a pest because the farmer grows his crops as densely as possible so making them an extremely rich and easily exploited feeding ground. The result is that animals which have lived innocuously on a variety of foods in the countryside may suddenly 'discover' a new source of food and overrun it.

Since about 1940 bullfinches have been a severe pest of English orchards. In normal circumstances bullfinches lead a retiring life in woodlands. They keep to the foliage and only their white rump gives them away. Their food for most of the year consists of seeds, particularly those of six species: ash, birch, privet, bramble, dock and nettle. As the seeds begin to run out in late winter and spring, the bullfinches supplement their rations with buds until the new seed crop is formed. If there is an orchard nearby, the bullfinches leave the woods and attack the buds of orchard trees. A single bull-finch can destroy 30 buds a minute and, as it eats only the centre of each bud, it has to eat a large number to get any sustenance. It only takes a few days for a flock of a dozen birds to reduce the eventual crop of an orchard to a few pounds of fruit.

The supply of seeds eaten by bullfinches in wood-land, varies from one winter to the next and, conse-quently, the damage to fruit trees also varies. When seeds are plentiful the bullfinches stay in the woods and damage to the buds of fruit trees is negligable, but when the seed crop fails, the bullfinches are forced out of the woods and into the orchards. Ash seeds are the bullfinches' most important food and the ash crop fails on alternate years. Records from fruit-growers show that, over the years, bullfinch attacks are serious on alternate years, coinciding

The male Common crossbill *Loxia curvirostris* use crossed ▷ mandibles of the bill to extract seeds from cones. As the crop of cones varies from year to year in different places, crossbills are nomadic. They move around until they find an area with a good cone crop and spend the rest of the year there.

oak-hickory climax forest

pine forest

grasses and shrubs

grasses

weeds

Grasshopper sparrow

Meadow lark

Field sparrow

Pine warlber   towhee   cardinal

Carolina wren   Wood thrush
Hooded warbler   Red-eyed vi

time in years since abandonment of field

1   5   15   25   50   100

with the failure of the ash crop. A possible solution to the bullfinch problem is to find a way of ensuring that there is a good supply of seeds every year but Ian Newton, who discovered these facts, has pointed out that this would mean that an increasing number of bullfinches would survive the winter because usually the population is kept in check by a high death rate in years of scarcity. An enlarged population would then become a more serious pest. Killing bullfinches in the spring when they are doing the damage has little effect because they are replaced by more bullfinches coming out of the woods. The best time to control bullfinches is in the autumn. Large numbers die in the winter but,

if some are trapped in the autumn, there will be fewer birds to eat into the stock of seeds at the beginning of winter. The seeds will last longer and the surviving bullfinches will not have to forage for buds in the spring.

The careful study of the feeding regime of bullfinches has resulted in a method of control that is efficient and not too costly. Furthermore, by killing the birds which were going to die anyway during the winter, the numbers of a rather pretty bird have not been reduced. Killing individuals already condemned has, however, been found to be the stumbling block to the control of another pest species.

◁ Each kind of habitat has a variety of birds that are adapted for living there. Some species can live only in one particular habitat: others live in a selection of habitats. If the vegetation in an area changes, the species of birds living there will also change, those present at any time reflecting the nature of the vegetation. Over the last 200 years a considerable area of farmland in eastern and southeastern United States has been abandoned and gradually overgrown by forests. The resulting changes have led to colonization by different birds in increasing numbers.

A Crested tit *Parus cristatus* with a caterpillar ▷ destined for its chicks. Crested tits live almost exclusively in pinewoods, preferring mature stands, but occasionally they spread into neighbouring clumps of birch and alder. Their range in Scotland was severely limited by the extensive felling in the 17th and 18th centuries, but they are now slowly spreading as the reafforestation programme proceeds. Crested tits feed mainly on insects picked from pine trees. They hop around the trunks rather like treecreepers but they also eat seeds from pine cones and juniper berries.

The Old World nutcracker *Nucifraga caryocatactes* and Clarke's nutcracker *N. columbiana* of western North America split open the nuts of hazel and the seeds of conifers. There is a projection in the lower half of the bill which fits into a cavity of the upper half to make efficient nutcrackers.

The Wood pigeon, like the bullfinch, lives in woods but descends on crops to feed. It attacks grain, clover and brassica crops. Also like the bullfinch, large numbers of Wood pigeons die in winter through shortage of food. When there is snow and frost on the ground Wood pigeons can be seen flapping about, unable to fly. If picked up, they will be found to be completely emaciated; there is no flesh left on them. For many years it was the practice in Europe to hold winter shoots, firing at the pigeons as they flew into their roosts. The authorities gave financial support to the shoots but, unfortunately, the venture was not successful. Close study of Wood pigeon populations has shown that numbers reach a peak when the young fledge. During the winter, many of the pigeons die because there is not enough food to support the large population. The effects of the winter pigeon shoots was to remove no more than the proportion of pigeons that would have died anyway through starvation. Indeed, shooting could, paradoxically, increase their numbers, because, as with the bullfinches, killing some pigeons early in the winter leaves more food for the remaining birds, allowing more of them to survive the rest of the winter.

Man has been acting as an important predator of the bullfinch and the Wood pigeon yet he has had no significant effect on their numbers. The moral is that, in many cases, predators do not affect the numbers of their prey. They are only killing those that are going to die of starvation. Food is the lynch-pin of survival, not 'nature red in tooth and claw'. As a corollary, the best way of improving stocks of gamebirds is not to kill off the vermin but to improve the birds' food supply. The 'vermin' may even be useful. They probably kill the weaker or injured birds, so conserving food for the stronger ones.

Territories and Colonies

One of the fundamental concepts in zoology is that of territory. A brief definition is that a territory is an area defended by an animal against members of its own species, so that it can search for food and rear its young without interference from its neighbours. The value of such an area can be appreciated if one compares a family having tea on the lawn of their back garden with a family picnicking on a crowded beach. In the former case the family is secure in their territory. There is room for the children to play without becoming lost or coming into conflict with neighbouring families, and the tea things can be laid out without fear of their being kicked over or pilfered. Territory then, is an animal's 'home', but the further the subject has been investigated the more complex it proves to be.

The idea of animals having a territory or home is not new. Aristotle was aware that eagles held territories, but the importance of territories was brought to the fore by a British amateur ornithologist, Eliot Howard. Howard's interest lay in the study of warblers. These are small, drab birds that skulk amongst the foliage of trees and shrubs or in undergrowth and herbage. They would be quite inconspicuous if it were not for their pleasant trilling songs. Indeed, many of them are most easily identified by their songs. Gilbert White of Selborne was the first person to properly distinguish the chiffchaff, Willow warbler and Wood warbler. The first two are virtually indistinguishable in appearance but there is no chance of confusing the almost monotonous *chiff-chaff-chiff-chiff* of the chiffchaff and the liquid trill rippling down the scale of the Willow warbler.

Territory and the Reed Warbler. The warblers start to sing in spring when the trees are still bare of leaves. This is the start of the breeding season, when the birds stop concentrating merely on their personal survival and start preparations for making good their numbers after the winter's losses. Howard watched male Reed warblers return from their winter quarters in Africa and take up residence in the reed beds bordering streams and lakes. At first the warblers go about in flocks, but then individual males leave the flock and retire to a patch of reeds where they sing. Over a period, the males spend more and more time away from the flock, until the flock no longer exists and each male has its own patch which it defends against other males. During this period they sing intensively, while they flit from reed to reed. They also chase and fight any other males that dare to cross the territory boundary.

The repeated singing and boundary disputes serve to 'beat the bounds' of the various territories so that each Reed warbler learns the extent of its own and its neighbours' property. As the boundaries become established, the amount of singing and fighting dies down. It is at about this time that the female warblers arrive from the winter quarters. The males are now ready to court the females by enticing them into the territories. After forming a bond with a male, the females, too, learn the boundaries and help in their defence.

Within the confines of the territory, each pair of Reed warblers builds a nest, the female doing most of the work, and raises a family of chicks. The food of the adults and chicks is insects and their

The Sage grouse *Centrocercus urophasianus* lives in the semi-desert sagebrush country of western North America. The male Sage grouse has elaborate plumage and ornaments for display. He erects his pointed tail feathers, puffs out his white chest, inflating two airsacs (not visible from the side) the colour and size of oranges. In this posture the head is almost hidden and the grouse struts about, uttering a 'popping' call. Such displays take place at 'strutting grounds', several hundred males sometimes gathering at a single strutting ground for a performance each morning and evening during the courtship season. The exact function of the displays is not altogether clear, but they may help bring the male into breeding condition.

larvae, such as the dragonflies, midges and Stone flies that inhabit reed beds. It would seem, then, that the territory of the Reed warbler supplies all its needs. The defended boundaries keep other Reed warblers away so that the owner and his mate can court and rear their young in peace. It is obviously an advantage to be able to carry out the daily routine without disturbance. So the possession of territories keeps a population well spaced out. It also causes the food supply to be divided fairly evenly amongst the breeding pairs.

More recent research has shown that the story outlined above is an oversimplification, for it appears that Reed warblers obtain most of their food from neutral ground outside the territory. Furthermore, Reed warblers can set up territories and breed successfully outside the reed beds. Some other uses of Reed warbler territories have also come to light. The residents of a territory soon become familiar with its layout. They learn the positions of trees and other outstanding features, the best places for food and the best routes through the dense beds of reeds. Knowing where to search for food must become quite an important asset when there is a nestful of hungry beaks to fill, and it is likely that the warblers will have favourite feeding places outside the territory as well as within it. A good knowledge of the layout of the territory is also very useful when attacked by a predator. A blind rush for cover may result in the pursued animal becoming cornered and caught, but if it is familiar with its surroundings, it can slip rapidly through dense cover while its pursuer is left floundering. This applies to many animals, from warblers flitting into the cover of a reed bed to deer and rabbits running helter-skelter along woodland tracks, and there is some evidence, gained mainly from the study of caged animals, that an animal will take great pains to learn as much as possible about an area when it is first introduced into it.

A male Superb lyrebird *Menura novaehollandiae* in full display. The 'lyre' is formed from the ornate tail which is 30 in (76 cm) long. There are two ribbon-shaped outer feathers forming the frame of the lyre, with two black wire-like feathers and 12 silvery filamentous feathers between them.

Hanging nests of weaverbirds in an Acacia tree. Most weavers are gregarious. They feed on seeds in flocks and nest in colonies. The plumage of the sexes are generally alike. Territorial behaviour consists of displays in which ownership of the nest is indicated by signals.

The Effect of Spacing-out. It has been found that when a bird has discovered a certain item of food it will start to search nearby for more. For instance, a tit or a jay may find a caterpillar as it searches through the foliage of a tree. It will then search particularly for these caterpillars. The more it finds, the more intense will its search become. On the other hand, if its search meets with little success it loses interest and moves elsewhere. From the point of view of the predator this is an efficient system; it makes the most of a concentration of food, but does not waste time on a scanty supply. It follows that it is to the advantage of the prey animal to be spaced out, so that the predator's appetite does not become whetted. As a result of living in territories, Reed warblers are spaced out in such a way as to preclude the possibility of any predator killing off the entire colony.

The effect of spacing-out on the behaviour of predators and their success at finding food is enhanced by their prey resorting to camouflage. This subject will be discussed later but, in brief, those birds with large territories and well spaced nests tend to have concealed nests. The nests of pipits are built under heather or herbage and are virtually impossible to find unless one comes so close as to scare the sitting bird into rising. Even then, the shock of the bird flying up is often sufficient to

distract one's attention from the exact spot from which it flew. Female ducks are also well camouflaged in comparison to the gaudy males, and they, too, sit tight on their eggs.

Clustering for Protection. In contrast to birds that live in large territories, many seabirds live in large, densely-packed colonies. The nests are set close together and the birds show no attempt at camouflage. Colonies of gulls, gannets, terns, albatrosses and penguins can be seen, heard and even smelt from a great distance. Clearly territory must have a different role in these species.

The territorial systems of gulls and their relatives have received particular attention from ornithologists. In these birds, as in other seabirds, the territory has no significance as a source of food. They get their food from the sea where there is plenty for all, and members of a colony may feed reasonably peacefully together, then return to the colony in company. Small groups of albatrosses and gannets can be seen gliding in close formation to their cliff-top colonies, where each one settles at its nest and promptly becomes bitterly jealous of its neighbours.

The territory of these birds is often no more than a rough circle whose radius is the distance that a bird can jab with its bill while sitting on its nest. Thus, two Adélie penguins will scream at each

European robin *Erithacus rube-cula* in flight. The robin is a pugnacious defender of its territory. Neighbours are dissuaded from entering the territory by a sweet liquid song and by displays in which the red breast is exposed to best advantage. If these warnings do not succeed a fight ensues. The robin is unusual in that both sexes have bright plumage and the female joins in the defence of the territory. Furthermore, both sexes defend territories during the winter. The European robin was originally called the red-breast. Later it became Robin redbreast and was then contracted to robin. The name has been applied to red-breasted birds around the world. The American robin is a thrush and, like its European relative, it is a familiar garden bird.

other with necks outstretched and bills only an inch or so apart. At the beginning of the nesting season a penguin may get forced out of position. It gets attacked vigorously by its neighbours, who beat it with their flippers. During the commotion other penguins become displaced and the conflict spreads until the contestants get properly spaced again. On some rocky islands, there is a limited amount of space for nesting so that the birds have to nest close together. Spectacular colonies of gannets, or cliff ledges packed with razorbills and guillemots, are illustrations of this need but the equally spectacular colonies of penguins or albatrosses that occupy only a small part of the ground available for nesting suggest that there are factors at work that promote gregariousness. It would seem that these species find that the advantages of nesting in tight groups are somehow sufficiently worthwhile to overcome the disadvantages of such a communal life.

The Fraser Darling Effect. In 1939, F. Fraser Darling propounded a theory that explained the advantages of nesting in colonies. He suggested that a bird is stimulated by the behaviour of its neighbours so that there is a mass effect bringing the members of a colony into the correct physiological condition for courtship and egg-laying at approximately the same time. Courtship displays and calls, it seems, have an effect on more than a bird's prospective mate. They act on all the other

birds so that each one excites the others and affects their reproductive organs and glands. As a result, the members of a colony lay their eggs within the space of a few days.

Fraser Darling got his idea from studying colonies of Herring and Lesser black-backed gulls. He found that gulls in the larger colonies, where there is more mutual stimulation, laid their eggs in a shorter period than in the smaller ones. Moreover, a greater proportion of the chicks survived in the larger colonies. When gull chicks are very small they are eaten by other gulls, crows and sometimes herons or other large birds but, once their feathers begin to sprout, they are reasonably safe. The predators can take only a certain number of chicks each day so, if all the chicks in a colony are vulnerable during one restricted period, the predators can take fewer of them. A gull is likely to lose its chicks if they hatch earlier or later than the majority of the colony. Natural selection will, therefore, act in favour of those gulls that lay at the same time as most other members of the colony. The social stimulation leading to synchronized breeding in colonial birds is sometimes called the 'Fraser Darling effect'. Some other studies have produced contradictory evidence but it could well be that there are different factors acting on other species and they would gain less advantage from synchronized breeding.

Once a species has obtained an advantage from

Wood warbler *Phylloscopus sibilatrix* at its domed nest among bracken. Wood warblers live in mature woodland where the canopy of leaves hinders the undergrowth. They feed on insects plucked from leaves while hovering. Insects are supplemented with berries just before their autumn migration to Africa. The drab plumage of warblers make them difficult to identify in the field. Gilbert White of Selborne was the first person to distinguish the Wood warbler, the Willow warbler and the chiffchaff. They are most easily told apart by their songs. The Wood warbler has two songs. One is a repeated single note that speeds to a trill and the second is a repeated, plaintive *pee-ur*. The songs may be heard in the winter quarters and on migration but Wood warblers are most vocal during the nesting season. The male sings while moving about in the tree canopy or while in flight. His songs advertize his presence to other Wood warblers, which might not be able to see him amongst the foliage. The songs serve to mark out the territories of the Wood warblers. They act as an audible warning for other males to keep away but also to entice unmated females. The latter arrive from Africa only after the territories have been established so they can immediately start courtship. The male Wood warbler courts by flying in front of the female with rapidly beating wings or with long, slow wingbeats like a butterfly.

nesting in colonies it has to evolve ways of avoiding the disadvantages. The 'Fraser Darling effect' minimizes predation on chicks by aerial hunters, but the main protection of the adults as well as the broods, is gained from the fact that colonial birds usually nest in inaccessible places where there are few predators. Seabirds often nest on remote rocks or islets and the colonial weaverbirds of Africa nest in trees. Those that are vulnerable, such as gulls and terns which nest on accessible sand banks or grassland, protect themselves by flying from the nest when a predator, such as a fox, approaches the colony. The eggs are camouflaged and the predator is distracted from its search by the adult birds 'stooping' at it, that is diving repeatedly at its head and sometimes hitting it with their feet. Colonial birds that do not have camouflaged eggs sit firmly on the nest when there is a predator about. Penguins stay on the nest when skuas attempt to steal their eggs and the closely packed nests make it difficult for an attacking skua to avoid being pecked by the penguins.

Another disadvantage to be overcome when living in a colony is caused by neighbouring pairs of birds living very close to each other. They may have a strict boundary between their small territories but they are still very much aware of the presence of their neighbours. If pairs of Reed warblers or blackbirds were forced into close proximity there would be so much friction that nesting would be impossible, but the colonial species have developed ways of reducing boundary fights. Instead of fighting, they warn trespassers by means of displays and calls; their aggression has been 'ritualized' from physical combat to a series of gestures. In human terms it is the substitution of diplomacy for war.

Size of Territory. The area that a bird has to defend if it is to raise a brood successfully varies enormously from species to species. In general the predatory birds, which need a hunting ground, have the largest territory. The Golden eagle has the largest territory on record: in California each pair held an area of 36 sq mi (93 sq km). At the other end of the scale are the colonial nesting birds that require only enough space in which to build their nests. European Black-headed gulls defend less than 5·4 sq ft (0·5 sq m) and for hole-nesters, such as House sparrows and starlings the nest site forms the whole territory.

Territory size also varies within a single species. If numbers are low a pair can hold as much territory as it needs and there may be a strip of no-man's-land between territories. In this situation neighbouring pairs may never meet and boundary disputes do not occur. As numbers rise, boundaries become clearly marked out and conflict arises as each pair seeks to retain its property. Eventually there comes a limit below which the size of a territory cannot drop. Below this limit a territory will not be able to provide all the essential services required by a pair to rear its brood.

Ovenbird *Seiurus aurocapillus*, one of the American warblers or wood-warblers. They are classed in a separate family from the Old World warblers and the ovenbird is not related to the South American ovenbirds that make domed nests of sticks and mud. The ovenbird lives in woodlands. It spends its time on the ground and walks rather than hops. It constructs its domed nest of leaves on the ground. It prefers woodland with a good cover of undergrowth and it is more often heard than seen. The degree of cover is important and ovenbirds are able to hold smaller territories in open aspen forests, where there is plenty of undergrowth, than in dense forests where the ground is bare.

Gannets *Sula bassana* nest on steep islands and rocks. The cliff ledges and tops are packed with nests of rotten seaweed and cliff plants.

The territory of the North American ovenbird, one of the Wood warblers and not to be confused with the South American ovenbirds, varies from 186,200 sq ft (17,400 sq m) to 34,240 sq ft (3,200 sq m). The size depends on the type of forest in which the ovenbird lives. The territory is smallest in aspen forests, where the trees are low and scattered and there is plenty of undergrowth, and is largest in maple forests where the tall trees and their dense canopies hinder the growth of ground vegetation. The variation in territory size may be due merely to the abundance of food, as in the Pomarine skua (known in America as the Pomarine jaeger) which lives almost exclusively on lemmings. Lemmings are well known for the way that their numbers rise to a high peak then collapse in the space of a few years. In 1952 lemmings were scarce and the Pomarine skuas defended territories of nearly 5 million sq ft (450,000 sq m). The following year, there was a surge in the abundance of lemmings and the size of skua territories dropped to under a million sq ft (80,000 sq m).

91

◁ Greenfinches *Carduelis chloris* fighting. Usually this species is sociable and tolerant of its fellows. At the end of summer greenfinches gather in flocks to feed on fallen seeds or to visit bird tables. They also roost in groups of up to 50 individuals.

Common guillemots or ▷ murres *Uria aalge* nest in thousands on cliff ledges. These birds are nesting on the sea cliffs of Svalbard where guillemots and other auks nest by the million. After spending the winter at sea, guillemots arrive at their breeding colonies and perform communal displays on the sea and in the air.

For many birds, the territory is independent of food supply but, even where it is not, there are other characters that affect its size. There has to be a suitable nest-site; a hole for Pied flycatchers or a cliff ledge for Peregrine falcons. The need for a nest-site explains the popularity of nest boxes for tits and other birds. In the modern well-kept countryside, old trees, where natural holes occur, are not often tolerated. It also explains why kingfishers may nest some distance from water. They need a stretch of water for fishing, but also need an earthy bank for a nest burrow. A stream or lake with low banks does not provide this second need and the kingfisher has to commute from nest to feeding ground.

Courtship Territories. So far, a territory has been considered as a place where a bird builds its nest and raises its brood, but there are territories which are not used for nesting. In many members of the grouse family, such as the capercaillie, Black grouse and Prairie chicken, and among some waders, the manakins, birds-of-paradise and others, the territories are strictly for the males. During the mating season they gather in traditional display grounds called arenas, hills or dancing-grounds, according to the species. Each male owns a small area, called a court or lek, where he displays vigorously to the other males. In this activity he is aided by an ornate plumage or a loud voice. The drab females come to the arenas to pick a mate and, after mating, they leave to rear a brood in seclusion.

The courts of the grouse and the ruff are small patches of ground, those of the ruff being only a foot or so in diameter, but some 'lek birds' have more elaborate courts. The male cock-of-the-rock, a cotinga of tropical South American forests, has a special perch where it waits for the female to arrive. When she appears at the arena, the males descend from their perches and display on the courts, which are patches of ground cleared of leaves.

The bowerbirds of New Guinea and Australia have the most elaborate courts of all. The early European explorers thought that they must have been made by the aboriginals. The courts or 'bowers' come in several forms. There are avenues enclosed by parallel walls of twigs or wigwams of sticks erected around a sapling. The bowers are elaborately decorated with leaves, feathers, flowers, dead insects and other objects. Nowadays, paper, empty tins, broken glass and other rubbish are used. Some bowerbirds even paint their bowers with the juices of berries or with charcoal mixed with saliva. A piece of bark is used as a paintbrush. It takes a male bowerbird several years to perfect his building technique but he is then ready to lure a female into his bower and to mate with her. Afterwards, she raises a brood by herself.

Winter Territories. The European robin, blackbird and Great grey shrike and the Plain tit, Loggerhead shrike and Red-headed woodpecker of America defend territories throughout the winter. The Loggerhead shrike and the woodpecker have

King penguins *Aptenodytes patagonica* at their breeding ground on South Georgia. The colonies usually contain several thousand pairs. Like the Emperor penguin, the King penguin makes no nest but balances the egg on its feet. It differs from the Emperor penguin in that it holds a small territory.

winter territories separate from the summer breeding territory. Why these birds should defend winter territories is not clear. One suggestion is that, by holding its territory over the winter, a male is sure of having a territory for the next breeding season. This may be so for the blackbird but in robins, the hens as well as the cocks hold territories and advertize their presence by singing. The territories will supply a large amount of food during the winter as in the case of the Red-headed woodpecker which uses its winter territory for storing acorns. It defends the territory against its fellows and against possible robbers such as jays. However, both robin and blackbird feed outside their winter territories in bad weather. Furthermore, the need for a winter territory to ensure food supply cannot be overwhelming because hen blackbirds survive without winter territories. As with other aspects of bird biology research has yielded much information on territorial behaviour but it continues to pose even more problems on the function and advantages of such behaviour.

Birdsong

The use of sound as a means of communication has been developed to a greater extent in birds than in any other animal except man and perhaps the dolphins and whales. Vocal communication is particularly well developed in one group of the passerine birds, the oscines or songbirds. The songbirds are responsible for the sounds that are popularly called birdsong but it is not always easy to distinguish between songs and other calls, and songs are by no means confined to the songbirds. The question of what is a song and what is a songbird cannot be answered simply. The answer depends on whether a song is to be defined, anthropomorphically, as a collection of rhythmic notes pleasing to the human ear or whether it is to be defined, biologically, by its function in a bird's life.

Function of Song. Some birds have a variety of calls; the chaffinch, a notable songbird, has 14 but some gulls, which are not songbirds, also have a variety. Each call has a function. There are contact calls which keep members of a flock or a family together, the begging calls of chicks and alarm calls which give warning of danger. Other calls indicate the position of a supply of food, a roost or a nest-site. The songs of birds differ from their other calls in volume, persistence and rhythmicity. The pattern of notes in a song is pleasing to human ears, and it has been suggested that men learned to sing by listening to the birds, but aesthetic value does not define song. The monotonous call of the cuckoo or the metallic notes of some barbets, known as Brain-fever birds because of their maddening regularity, are songs in the strict sense. They have little or no musical quality but have the same function as the most melodious songs. Although it is not impossible that some birds get pleasure from their

Reed bunting *Emberiza schoeniclus* singing from the top of a bramble. It is found mainly in marshes and in the vegetation lining the banks of rivers and ponds but recently it has colonized dry places. The song of the Reed bunting is a weak but persistent twittering. The advertizing message of the song is reinforced by the bunting's habit of making itself conspicuous through singing from an exposed perch or while flying. Reed buntings sing most persistently in February and March, before the females arrive from the winter quarters. Singing then falls off but a male will start to sing while his mate is away from the territory.

songs, they have, primarily, a strictly utilitarian function. The singer is stating clearly that he owns a territory: males must keep away but unattached females are welcome. The song is an audible advertizement and it follows that it must be loud and repeatedly uttered so that other birds can learn the position of the singer. Songs are often loudest and most prolonged among woodland birds, the wrens for instance, where dense undergrowth prevents neighbours from seeing each other. In more open country, the song may be supported by the use of trees or bushes as regular singing posts or by song-flights. Pipits and larks habitually fly up as they sing. The skylark is particularly well known for a sustained warbling that regularly lasts for over 10 minutes as it climbs until it is no more than a speck in the sky.

The form of tune of a song must convey a further message: the identity of the singer. It must indicate his species and his individual identity. Songs are often the best way of identifying a bird, particularly in woodland, and people with a good 'ear' can sometimes identify particular birds. The 'tune' is the same in all but slight variations in pitch and timing allow individuals to be recognized. A song may be instinctive or learned by imitation, but each bird grows up with the correct form of communication for spacing out males of its own species or attracting the right mate. The Eastern and Western meadowlarks of North America have overlapping ranges and nest in the same habitat. They are very difficult to distinguish by appearance but can be easily identified by their songs. The Eastern meadowlark has a clear, four-note whistle while the Western species has a gurgling warble. Female meadowlarks are attracted to a male of the correct species by recognizing his song.

Song Structure. The range and complexity of many songs is far beyond the capability of the most perfect human voice and analysis has revealed complexities that cannot be appreciated by the most sensitive human ear. The European wren utters high pitched notes at a rate of over 10 per second, a fact that can only be appreciated if the song is played back on a recorder at slow speed. A sound spectrograph, a machine that prints out the frequencies of sounds as a 'picture' or spectrogram, can be used to analyse individual songs. Spectrograms of songs by birds of the same species show clearly the differences that allow individual birds to be recognized. For example, they have shown individual variations in the songs of finches.

Bird song is fundamentally different from the human voice, the difference lying in the anatomy of the sound-producing mechanism. The human voice is produced in the larynx, at the junction between the windpipe, or trachea, and the throat. The vocal cords are two folds that partially obstruct the larynx and vibrate when air is forced from the lungs, in much the same way as the lips can be made to vibrate by blowing through them. The frequency of the sound produced is regulated by the tension applied to the vocal cords by small muscles, and words are formed by changes in the position of the lips, jaws and tongue which alter the sounds as they pass through the mouth. In birds, the voice comes from the syrinx, an organ lying at the junction between the trachea and the bronchi which lead from the lungs. Its structure is roughly the same as that of the larynx in that sound is produced by vibrating membranes, but it is more complex. In each bronchus there is a vibrating membrane that forms a wall between the bronchus and one of the airsacs of the breathing system. Opposite this membrane is a moveable labium. To sing, a bird squeezes the airsac by contracting its chest muscles. The pressure forces the membrane across the bronchus to form a valve. Muscles then draw back the membrane and air rushes past, making it vibrate. The frequency of the vibrations depends firstly on the size of the opening, which is controlled by the muscles of the syrinx altering the tension on the membrane, and secondly by the position of the labium.

The tongue and the mouth are not used to modify the sounds as in human speech and the variety of bird song is due to the intricate structure of the syrinx, its associated muscles and the double nature of the mechanism. Some outstanding feats are achieved. For example, there is an independently vibrating membrane in each of the bronchi so birds can sing two tunes at once. Reed warblers and Brown thrashers produce overlapping songs, in which notes from one song are uttered at the same time as notes of the other. The Gouldian finch, a gorgeously coloured weaver-finch of the family Estrildidae, sings three songs simultaneously, consisting of a continuous, bagpipe-like drone overlain by two independent chirping tunes. The Wood thrush of North America sometimes utters four notes at once but how this is managed is not known.

Some modification of the sounds can be produced by the trachea or accessory airsacs to make deep, booming notes. Male Sage grouse inflate the large

Greater spotted woodpecker *Dendrocopos major* feeding its young. It is clinging to the tree trunk with its sharp claws, showing how two toes face forwards and two face back, and is propped by its stiff tail. The 'song' of many woodpeckers is a mechanical sound, made by drumming on wood with the bill. Both sexes of the Greater spotted woodpecker drum. They beat rapidly on a branch or trunk of a tree with the bill. The resulting harsh rattle can be heard quarter of a mile away. Each drum lasts for a second and its pitch depends on the diameter of the branch. Dead branches seem to be preferred and metal objects are sometimes used. Apparently a woodpecker will test branches with a few taps before deciding on a suitable site for drumming. At one time is was thought that drumming was vocal but ciné films have shown it to be caused by blows of the bill. The head of a woodpecker is adapted for chiselling holes in wood. The bill is strong with a sharp tip, the skull is strengthened, the nostrils are covered with feathers to keep out wood dust and the long neck has powerful muscles to deliver the hammer-blows.

yellow throat-pouches that form part of the breeding display and use them as resonators to enhance their loud, popping calls. Trumpeter swans, Whooping cranes, the Australian Trumpeter manucode (a bird-of-paradise) and the Plains chachalaca, produce deep, trombone-like calls through their lengthened trachea. That of the Whooping crane is 5 ft (1·5 m) long, of which half is coiled under the breastbone. The extra loop in the windpipe of the male chachalaca gives it a call one octave below that of the female. It has been suggested that the origin of the 'swan-song', the idea that a swan sings just before its death, is based on the final expirations of breath producing a wailing noise in the long windpipe.

There appears to be no relation between the complexity of the syrinx and the power of song. The true songbirds are distinguished from other birds by the number and complexity of the muscles regulating the membranes in the syrinx. Nevertheless, a complex syrinx does not necessarily confer powers of song. Crows, which are true songbirds on the basis of the musculature of the syrinx, are hardly musical, nor are the cuckoos and barbets with their monotonous calls. It is safest to define song in the context of behaviour: advertizing the possession of territory and readiness to mate. Songs can consequently be tuneless calls or even silent postures. Among the gull family, for instance, the displays used for territorial advertizement are often referred to as the 'song'. This is an instance of a word in everyday use having its meaning partly altered when used as a technical term. 'Song' now has rather different meanings to a layman and an ornithologist, the latter thinking more of territorial advertizement than of music. However, as the technical use is derived from the lay use there is considerable overlap and both are usually talking about the same sounds when they refer to birdsong. The technical meaning of song has even been used to describe the advertizing behaviour of mammals which, with the exception of the howls of the dog family and Howler monkeys and the trills of Weddell seals, is rarely composed of sound signals and more often of displays or scent marks.

Instrumental Song. Some birds have abandoned vocal songs for instrumental music. That is, they use the bill, wings or tail for sound production. Sounds made with the bill include the 'clappering' of storks, a staccato click by the Wandering albatross during courtship, and a loud snapping by Tawny and Eagle owls when disturbed. Some of the woodpeckers drum on trees with their bills. The Greater spotted woodpecker drums at a rate of up to 10 beats a second, producing a hollow rattle, sometimes described as sounding like a stick being

A Common snipe *Gallinago gallinago* on water plants by Lake Naivasha, Kenya. The species is widely distributed throughout the northern hemisphere, Africa and South America. Snipe become active at dusk during the breeding season. It can then be heard calling with a rhythmically 'jick-jack' and producing its drumming or bleating. The drumming is a mechanical noise made by the vibration of two modified outer tail feathers in the wind as it flies. These two feathers are held out from the rest of the tail as the bird dives at an angle of about 45°. The wing movements deflect puffs of air over the feathers to produce a quavering effect. The feathers are stiffer than the other tail feathers; the vane is made up of stiff barbs that can be easily separated from each other. Both male and female Common snipe indulge in drumming. The habit is found in other species of snipe but not in the Great snipe or Jack snipe.

The Indian hill mynah *Gracula religiosa* is a notable mimic, famous particularly for its 'wolf-whistles'. Yet mynahs have never been heard to mimic other species in the wild, they only copy other mynahs. In solitary captivity they cannot do this and take to mimicking other sounds. This behaviour contrasts with mockingbirds, lyrebirds and even the common starling which incorporate the sounds of other birds and the mechanical sounds of human activity into their songs. Captive mynahs seem to be best at mimicking sounds that resemble their calls, such as swear words and whistles.

drawn rapidly along wooden palings. Both sexes indulge in drumming and perform most frequently during the courtship period. For some time there was an argument as to whether the drumming sound was caused by pure percussion of the bill on wood or whether it was vocal, the wood acting as a sounding board. Drumming is difficult to observe closely but cine films have shown conclusively that the bill does make contact with the wood. The action is the same as in chiselling holes to extract grubs, but the blows in drumming are much more rapid and are delivered with far less force. Yet the sound of drumming carries up to a quarter of a mile (0·4 km), about 20 times the distance of sounds made in the forceful chiselling of wood in search of food. There seems to be no explanation for this.

Simple sounds made by clapping the wings are used in the courtship displays of nightjars, pigeons and owls. The Ruffed grouse 'booms' by striking its wings against its breast, but some male manakins have modified flight feathers which produce sounds when they are snapped together or when they are allowed to vibrate in the slipstream during flight. The American woodcock uses similarly stiffened and narrowed flight feathers to produce a whistling as it dives and soars during courtship and the snipes drum or bleat with stiffened tail feathers. In the European snipe, the tail is fanned and the two outer feathers are detached from the rest so that they can vibrate freely. As the bird dives at a steep angle, the wing movements deflect puffs of air over the tail feathers which vibrate in bursts to produce a quavering noise, rather like someone blowing across the top of an empty bottle in short puffs.

The Season of Song. The production of song is under the control of the sex hormones. Female canaries injected with the male sex hormone, testosterone, sing like males. In birds, the gonads, that is the ovaries and testes, undergo a marked annual cycle of changes. Outside the breeding season they shrink away and lie dormant through the winter. In spring, the lengthening days reawaken them to activity. Testes may increase in size by a factor of 200 or 300 and the production of sex hormones stimulates the other activities of the

The Blue-winged kookaburra *Dacelo leachi* or Barking kookaburra is less well-known than the Laughing kookaburra *D. gigas.* They are large king-fishers that live in wooded country and feed mainly on land animals, eating insects, snakes and birds, only occasionally catching fish. Kooka-burras are renowned for their raucous laughing calls and the Blue-winged kookaburra also has a discordant scream. They have been called the Clock bird or Bushman's clock because their loud chorus starts regularly at dawn.

breeding season: occupation of a territory, court-ship and singing. The greatest volume of song is heard in the spring, when the establishment of territory and courtship are at their peak. After the eggs have been laid and the male is busy with parental duties, the amount of singing wanes and may stop altogether. By this time, song is no longer needed to attract a mate and there is less need to advertize territorial boundaries as neighbouring males will be familiar with them. Some continued singing will, however, serve to maintain the pair bond. When nesting has finished some birds that have stopped singing start to sing again and there may even be some courtship activity but this is short lived. A few continue to sing throughout the year, however. Wrens and mockingbirds, for ex-ample, sing all winter and female European robins sing to advertize their winter territories.

The close correlation between the seasonal development of the testes and the onset of singing in spring pinpoints a function of song that goes beyond the advertizement to other members of the same species. Song is important as a means of co-ordinating the breeding cycles of a mated pair. The song of the male, and probably of neighbouring males, stimulates the reproductive system of the female. How this works is not known but presum-ably the song acts on the hormone-secreting glands via the brain.

Singing by female birds is rare. There are those, like the robin and mockingbird, that hold territories and a few others sing at other times, but some fe-males sing duets with their mates. Duetting occurs in several unrelated birds, such as the African shrikes, motmots, barbets, ovenbirds and whip-birds. In some special cases, known as antiphonal singing, one bird gives a short burst of song and its mate replies, usually with a different song. In many antiphonal songs the timing of the two parts is so precise that it is impossible to tell by the ear alone that there is more than one bird singing. Analysis of a series of duets by a pair of Black-headed gonoleks, an African shrike, shows that the second bird took its time from the first note uttered by the first bird. Its timing was so accurate that it varied by no more than 24 thousandths of a second.

Duetting has been studied closely in the Aus-tralian Eastern whipbird, a relative of the babblers that hunts insects in the woods bordering the coast of eastern Australia. It is named after the song of the male which starts with a pure note that in-creases in intensity and ends with a sharp whip-

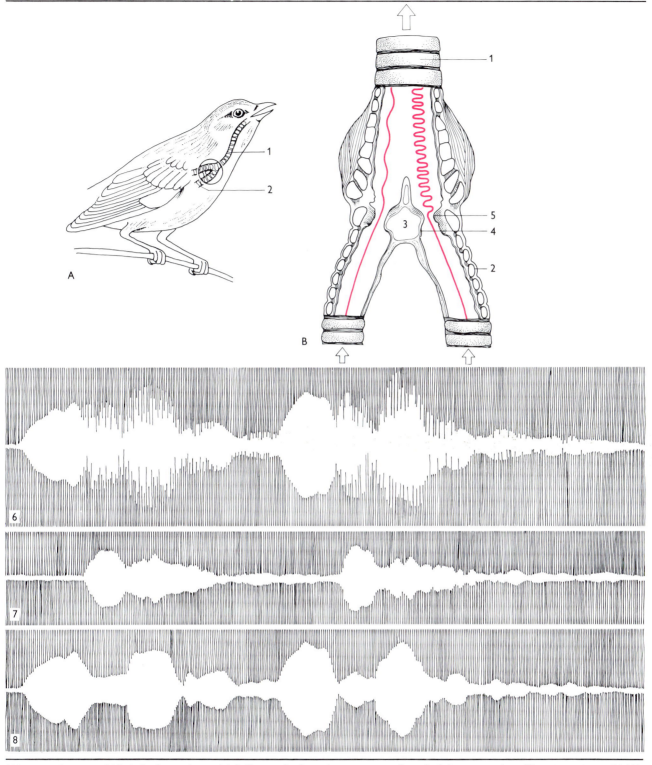

(A) The voicebox of birds is the syrinx, which lies at the junction between the windpipe or trachea (1) and the bronchi (2), tubes that lead to the lungs. In a vertical section through the syrinx (B), one can see an airspace (3) enclosed by the tympanic membranes (4), and two membranes called the external labia (5). Each external labium can be controlled independently. When air is forced past the gap between the tympanic membrane and external labium (left side), the tympanic membrane vibrates to produce sound. If the tympanic membrane is tensed against the pressure in the air sac (right side) the vibrations are of higher frequency and a higher note is produced. Sound frequency tracings of the song of a mocking bird during a period of $\frac{1}{3}$ of a second are shown in (C). In (6), the total song is recorded, while in (7) and (8), its separate components are shown. Each component is produced by separate external labia.

crack. The female replies with two or three notes. Whipbirds are shy, skulking birds of the undergrowth, characters they share with other duettists. It seems that one of the values of duetting is to inform each bird where its mate is, as well as to generally maintain the pair bond. The introductory note of the male whipbird is fairly quiet and has individual characteristics; it probably serves for recognition by the female. The whipcrack can be heard over a quarter mile (0.4 km) radius and has

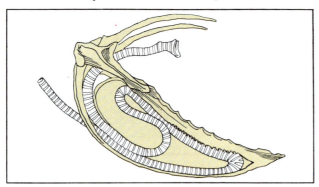

The long windpipe of a crane runs from the lungs, between the collar bones and lies coiled alongside the keel of the breastbone. In some cranes the windpipe may be 5 ft (1.5 m) long and penetrates the breast muscles. The long windpipe produces deep, trombone-like calls that can be heard up to 1 mi (1.6 km) away. In some cranes only the male has a lengthened windpipe.

physical characters that make it easy to locate. It, therefore, acts as a beacon which enables the female and other males locate the singer. The female's song is also easy to locate and serves to tell the male her position.

The Dawn Chorus. One of the most delightful activities of bird life, and one that still requires explanation, is the dawn chorus. It is the only compensation for a sleepless night when, in the early hours as the gloom of night gives way to dawn, the silence is broken by the first few bars of birdsong. Gradually the tempo and volume increase until the countryside is a babel of song. Every bird capable of singing seems to take part. Nothing like it can be heard at any other time and it lasts at its full intensity for about half an hour. Then it dies away and there is a period of silence until individual birds start singing again between the routine chores of feeding and parental duties. There is a low ebb of singing during the afternoon, particularly when nesting is under way, but towards sunset there is a renewed chorus of lesser intensity.

There is a pattern to the dawn chorus. As each bird awakes, it stretches itself, as do other awaken-

ing animals, preens and then flies to a song post. The first notes of song are fitful but gain in strength until the bird is singing for all its worth. It is not easy to tell how long each individual sings, but one European cuckoo, easily distinguished among the chorus by its peculiar *cuck-cuckoo* call, sang for nearly an hour. Its phrase was repeated every second, a monotonous 3,000 times before it fell quiet.

As the chorus builds up, other species can be heard chiming in and two hours may elapse between the first and last start singing. In Europe, the robin is often the first to start, but it is sometimes preceded by the cuckoo, blackbird or skylark. There appears to be some order in the start of singing. The European robin starts to sing about three minutes after awakening, the blackbird needs 5–6 minutes to start singing, while the chaffinch is a slow riser and is awake for 20 minutes before singing. In North America, the order of singing is Song sparrow, cardinal, robin. House wrens do not start until the light is quite bright.

The start of the dawn chorus is related to light intensity. It is earlier on fine mornings, especially if there is moonlight, than in overcast or rainy conditions. As spring progresses, the chorus beings earlier, not only in relation to the clock but to sunrise, which, itself, becomes earlier. In early spring, birds start to sing after sunrise, by midsummer they start before sunrise.

Despite detailed documentation of the dawn chorus and proof that it is triggered by light intensity, there seems to have been no good reason put forward as to why it should occur. There may be an advantage in birds letting each other know their position before beginning to move about, starting the day with a mass 'beating of the bounds' to ensure that territory boundaries are appreciated. Yet it is strange that there should be such a concerted outburst of song every morning. A good breakfast would seem to be a better way of starting the day and intermittent singing throughout the day sufficient to impress boundaries on the neighbours.

Mimicry. There are a surprising number of birds that display the power of vocal imitation in the wild. Starlings, catbirds, thrashers, birds-of-paradise and bowerbirds, all contrive to mix the songs of other species with their own. Other sounds are

The African grey parrot *Psittacus erithacus* is one of the ▷ most popular of parrots because it is such a good 'talker'. Although parrots may not know what they are saying they can often associate words and sounds with specific events.

also incorporated, including car horns, human conversation, dogs' barking, the sound of axes cutting wood and so on. The mockingbird is aptly given the scientific name of *Mimus polyglottos*, the many-tongued mimic. Its burbling, rapidly-changing song frequently includes snatches of song from several other species as well as mechanical sounds. When nightingales were brought from Europe to Florida the local mockingbirds imitated their songs with remarkable accuracy.

The biological function of mimicry is something of a mystery. Talking parrots have been popular since the time of the Ancient Greeks yet no one has ever heard them mimic other species in the wild. The same is true of the Indian hill mynah, a member of the starling family that challenges the parrots in popularity as a talker, although it is able to imitate other members of its own species. Some birds sing the right song by instinct. Others have to learn part or all of the song by hearing other birds of the same species. Chaffinches, for instance, sing only a shortened song if raised in isolation and never hear another chaffinch. Bullfinches also learn the songs of other bullfinches that they heard when young. It seems that mynahs, too, have to learn their songs by imitation of other mynahs. In captivity, they are denied this opportunity and have to use other sounds. The mimicking of human sounds comes readily because mynahs naturally produce sounds that have roughly the same frequency of the human voice and which are of short duration – like swear words or coughing.

It is often said that parrots or mynahs do not know what they are talking about; that they merely reel out sounds like a tape recorder. This is far from the truth, although they commonly pour out their repertoire in a meaningless jumble. There is ample evidence that they can fit sounds to the correct context, as birds must do in the wild if they are to give an alarm call or a begging call at the appropriate moment. A good parrot will say 'hello' repeatedly when a telephone rings or will bark as a dog goes past. It is easy, however, to overestimate the intelligence of a pet with which one is familiar; to say that a dog understands every word it hears, for instance. Yet it is difficult to accept the interpretation of the most elaborate mimicry of captive birds as being no more than part of the mechanism of learning the species' song. The parrot seems to take a very lively interest in its surroundings and seems to show some form of aesthetic sense in generating noises to match those it hears. Maybe this mimicry is a form of play, itself a little understood subject. Playful actions are often distortions of more prosaic actions, the play of cats being a distorted form of hunting for example. Play also seems to be a way of occupying empty time and gives the appearance of being enjoyable, two features which one might expect to see in the behaviour of cagebirds.

Courtship and the Pair Bond

Animals usually keep their distance from each other. Flocks of starlings feeding in a field, or swallows perched on a telegraph wire, are well spaced. If one bird comes too close to its neighbour, there is an altercation and they move apart but, for the continuance of the species, the two sexes must come together, if only to enable fertilization of the eggs. For some birds, this is the limit of contact. The female is attracted to a male, they mate, and she retires to lay eggs and rear the brood alone. In others, the sexes form a bond and share the parental duties. Sometimes the bond is retained for life. The essence of courtship is to remove the barriers between two individuals and allow them to come together. After the initial courtship is over, courtship activities continue at intervals to cement the bond that now holds the pair together. By retaining the bond from year to year the preliminaries of courtship can be reduced and breeding can get under way rapidly at the beginning of the season.

The Ritual of Courtship. The general pattern of courtship is for a male to signal to a female and entice her to him. The male bird starts to signal, in the form of songs or displays, when his reproductive system is in an active state and, in some birds, the male's signals trigger the development of the female's reproductive system to ensure that the sexes are brought together in a suitable state for fertilization to take place. In budgerigars, for instance, the soft warbling of the male causes the female's ovaries to develop and the eggs to form.

The male's courtship signals must also be species-specific, that is, they must act as signals only to females of the same species. Konrad Lorenz tells of a male Black stork and a female White stork that tried to mate in a cage at Schönbrunn zoo. The male displayed with sinuous movements of the neck, from side to side and up and down, and the female replied by clattering her bill and laying her neck over her back. Neither recognized the other's signals and their friendship never ripened. Courtship signals may even be needed to allow the sexes to be distinguished. As a preliminary to courtship, the male Adélie penguin lays a pebble at its mate's feet as a symbol of the pile of pebbles that will become the nest. A bachelor will lay its pebble at the feet of any likely-looking penguin. If it is a male or unreceptive female, the bachelor is pecked

Black-headed gull *Larus ridibundus* displaying in the 'forward posture'. It is an attitude used during territorial disputes to signal aggression. The chocolate-brown mask is, itself, an aggressive signal and is being presented fully to an opponent. The wings are held slightly open in readiness for a leap forward and, as such, are a signal to that effect.

Courtship feeding by the Little tern *Sterna albifrons*. Feeding of the female by the male during the courtship and incubation periods is a feature of the breeding behaviour of the terns and their relations, the gulls and skuas. In the terns the presentation of fish held in the bill has developed into a ceremony. At the start of the breeding season males carry fish around the colony and display to unmated females but do not relinquish their fish. Only when a pair is formed does feeding take place and it becomes more frequent as egg-laying approaches. After the eggs have been laid the male continues to feed the female at intervals until the chicks hatch out and both parents turn to feeding them. The value of courtship feeding lies in maintaining the bond between the two birds and in assisting the female in the formation of eggs. The ceremony of displaying fish in the early stages of courtship may enable a female tern to assess the male's potential as a provider.

but a receptive female responds favourably and both penguins indulge in mutual courtship displays, waving their heads from side to side with the bill pointed skywards. The mutual display is later used as a form of greeting whenever the pair meet. It helps to cement the bond and enables each to recognize the other.

With his songs and displays the male appears to take the initiative in courtship but the female has a far from passive role. The female makes the choice of a mate, not the male, and, if there are no differences in plumage, she may have to persuade him that she is a female and not a trespassing male. The male Song sparrow establishes a territory and sings with gusto to advertize his presence. He pounces on any female that enters his territory and knocks into her. If she is not searching for a mate she flees, otherwise she stands her ground and the male realizes her sex and courts her. A female gull has to be more positively submissive. She indicates her sex by approaching the male with an appeasement display. Her body is lowered and the neck withdrawn or bent so that she is looking up at the male. The Black-headed gull is named for the chocolate brown mask that both sexes assume in the breeding season. The mask acts as an aggressive signal and courting Black-headed gulls indulge in a 'head-flagging' display. Being unused to each others' proximity they start to threaten one another, then suddenly turn their heads away, so that they cannot see the offending mask. While facing away they are learning to tolerate each other. Male gannets sit on their newly built nests and display to passing females but, when one lands, the male, rather surprisingly, bites her neck. The female's reaction is to appease the male by turning away.

Differences in appearance makes courtship easier as the sexes can be distinguished from a distance without displaying. The male budgerigar has a blue patch at the base of the bill and the female has a brown patch. Males attack females painted blue and court males painted brown. Where there is no morphological distinction there are likely to be elaborate mutual displays. This is not always the case, but it is seen in many seabirds and geese and in the spectacular dance of the Great crested grebe. The grebes nest on lakes and, from mid-winter onwards, their displays can be seen until well into the spring. The unpaired bird draws attention to itself by loud croaking and, when joined by another, the dancing begins. The sexes' plumage is identical, both developing ear tufts and plumes during the breeding season, and either starts the courtship. One grebe dives under the other and rises vertically in the water. The other gives the 'cat-display', spreading the ear tufts to give it a rounded face and spreading the wings. After this, they 'head-shake', wagging their heads with plumes erect. This is the commonest display and is followed by the 'penguin dance', in which the pair rise breast-to-breast with lumps of weed in their bills, and by the 'retreat-ceremony' in which one bird runs across the water and subsides into the 'cat-display'. Other displays include offering the partner a fish.

Courtship Feeding. During the early stages of courtship, male cormorants, herons and storks give the female presents in the form of nest material. Later, this becomes part of the greeting ceremony and a stick may be removed from the nest and proffered as one bird arrives to relieve the other on the eggs. A more practical present is an offering of food. The male gives the female an item of food in the same way as they will later feed the chicks. The male kingfisher or tern gives a fish, the robin an insect, the bullfinch some seeds. Courtship feeding is to some extent part of the sequence leading to the formation and maintenance of the pair bond and may be formalized, so that the birds may go through the motions but do not actually exchange food. They may just touch bills and the European robin may beg for food even when her bill is already full of food for her nestlings.

Whatever the importance of courtship feeding psychologically, as part of pair bonding behaviour, it is certainly important to the female's reproductive physiology. The formation of a clutch of eggs imposes a great strain on a female bird. Among small birds a single egg may be 10 per cent of the adult's weight and the number laid will depend on the

Count Raggi's bird-of-paradise *Paradisea apoda reggiana* starts its display by spreading its wings and a fan of red flank plumes. As the display intensifies, the bird leans forward and flutters his wings so that the red plumes cascade over his head. At the same time he sings and females are attracted by the powerful and acoustic advertizement. In some species the males display communally, as many as 40 displaying in one tree. The females are drab brown and retire after mating to lay their eggs in seclusion. Very few bird-of-paradise nests have been found. Most are bowls of twigs perched on branches or rocks but one species lays its eggs in holes. The name *Paradisea apoda* commemorates the first appearance of birds-of-paradise in Europe. Magellan's expedition brought skins home in 1522 and the Spaniards felt that so fine a bird must have come from paradise. A trade in the skins sprung up and naturalists were surprised to find that they lacked legs. They decided that birds-of-paradise must spend their whole lives in the air, feeding on the dew of heaven. In fact, the legs had been removed to make packaging easier.

availability of food. The strain of egg production can be eased if the male saves the female the effort of foraging. The courtship of the Common tern consists of three phases. In the early stages, the males carry fish in their bills and display to the females. When the pair has formed they forage together and the male feeds his mate, supplementing the fish she catches herself. The third stage starts before egg laying. The female remains in the territory and has all her food brought to her. The more food the male brings, the larger eggs the female is able to lay. Consequently the chicks are larger and more likely to survive.

Courtship feeding is often continued through the incubation period until both parents have to concentrate on feeding the young. Even though both sexes in the gull family incubate and the female is free to feed herself every few hours she is still waited on by the male. Here, it would seem that maintaining the pair bond is important. Amongst the birds of prey, the female is the sole incubator. She may leave the nest on occasions to hunt for herself but the male is the main breadwinner. It is, however, more likely that the female only has to leave the nest when there is a shortage of food and the male cannot find enough for both. So there is a built-in safety mechanism to ensure that she gets enough food. If she does leave the nest, the eggs are left dangerously exposed to predation and fewer pairs breed successfully in lean years.

The harriers indulge in a spectacular feeding ceremony. The male calls the female from the nest and food is passed, either by the female taking it from the male's talons or by catching it in mid air after he has dropped it. The male continues to feed the female after the eggs have hatched; he has to provide food for himself and the whole of his family, at least until the young have grown their feathers.

Permanent Pairs. Among many birds the family splits up after the chicks have flown and even the parents may never see each other again, although they are both likely to return to the same area when the next breeding season comes round. Male songbirds are almost certain to pick roughly the same territory each year but it is only by chance that a female is attracted to last year's mate rather than to one of his neighbours. Finding the same mate is more likely if there is a definite draw to the same nesting site. Storm petrels and shearwaters retain the same mate more often than not in successive years because both return to the same nesting burrow at the beginning of the season.

Returning to the same mate, year after year, has advantages. Retaining the same nest-site saves time in searching and in collecting material or burrowing, and the time spent in courtship can be reduced. Young Wandering albatrosses spend several years visiting the breeding grounds before they lay. They spend this time procuring a mate and forging a

Copulation in the Arctic tern *Sterna paradisaea.* The male stands on the female's back, flapping his wings to keep his balance. Then he thrusts his tail down to bring the cloacas together for a few seconds.

The male Satin bowerbird *Ptilonorhynchus violaceus* builds a bower composed of a pad of sticks with a wall of sticks on each side. It is decorated with shells, flowers and dead insects and painted with plant juices.

bond. If one member of the pair later dies, its mate may take a year or more to form a bond with a new bird. If it takes so long to form a bond, it is obviously essential to keep the same mate from year to year. In other birds, such as kittiwakes, breeding success increases with the length of time that the pair have been together. They lay earlier, produce larger clutches and rear more young. Presumably, experience in some form is an asset in rearing a family and it is not too much to suggest that this is through the pair getting to know each others' ways.

The psychological nature of the pair bond in animals can only be guessed at, and to ascribe to animals any form of emotion leads one dangerously close to anthropomorphism. Nevertheless there are instances when it seems that the link between mates or the members of a social group go beyond the mechanistic processes required by reproductive or social biology. Among the mammals, with their advanced brain power, there are many stories of compassion and loyalty exhibited by primates, dolphins and dogs, but it occasionally appears that birds are not lacking in the emotions of fidelity or solidarity. It may just be a matter of an animal feeling at ease in the presence of a familiar companion. This might explain observations of Black ducks refusing to leave their mates after they had been shot, or the captive male magpie which, after its mate had died and its corpse removed, spent the next three days in the corner where it had lain.

Casual Mating. The advantages of a long-lived pair bond are of importance to birds in which both parents are needed to rear the chicks. There is little advantage for those birds whose chicks leave the nest almost immediately and feed themselves. Only a single parent is needed to incubate the young and guard the brood of chicks and the female

The Livingstone lourie *Tauraco livingstonii,* one of the turaco family of Africa. Other members of the family are known as plantain-eaters and Go-away birds, and they exhibit a variety of courtship displays. Bowing, raising the crest and displaying of the brilliantly coloured tail and wing feathers are all found in turacos.

The male peafowl *Pavo crista-tus*, known as the peacock, displays to the peahen. The peafowl is a member of the pheasant family in which it is usual for the male to have a showy plumage while the female is drab enabling her to be inconspicuous while sitting on the nest. The peacock's train is not the tail, as is sometimes thought, but is composed of up to 150 tail covert feathers that spring from the lower part of the back. The vanes of the feathers are loose, the barbules being unhooked so that the barbs stand by themselves. Normally the train hangs behind the peacock like a long bustle but it can be raised when the bird displays to a peahen or even to a human. Even the peahens and chicks will sometimes display their short tail coverts. Peacocks have been domesticated for over 2,000 years. They have been prized for their beauty and for their flesh. The Congo peacock was discovered only in 1936. It is the only pheasant found wild outside Asia.

usually fills this role, although there are interesting exceptions. The emancipation of the male leaves him free to concentrate on the territorial and courtship aspects of breeding behaviour. Being freed from incubation duties, he can lose his camouflaged plumage and develop gaudy plumes for showing off, while his territory need no longer contain a food supply and nest-site and can shrink to a small display ground. Such a pattern can be seen among the ducks, for example the mallard and eider, the manakins of South America, some waders, the bowerbirds, the birds-of-paradise and the gamebirds. The birds-of-paradise in particular, show extreme development of an ornate plumage in the males. The King of Saxony bird-of-paradise was discovered in a Paris market in 1840 at a time when there was a brisk trade in bird-of-paradise feathers for millinery. Ornithologists thought at first that the plumage had been made up by an unscrupulous dealer because two plumes, over twice the length of the bird, trailed like bunting from the head. The 'flags' were blue one side and brown the other. Other species have similarly bizarre plumages. They flaunt them at the display grounds, sometimes hanging upside down, and the females come to make their choice. The monogamous pair bond has been

lost in these birds and is replaced by promiscuous mating. After mating, the females leave the display ground to rear a family by themselves. They are extremely drab and, while the males are well known, the nests of many birds-of-paradise have yet to be found.

Polygyny and Polyandry. Casual mating is usually only possible when food is abundant and the chicks are relatively independent soon after hatching. It is restricted mainly to certain families but polygyny, the mating of one male with several females, sometimes occurs among usually monogamous birds. There was a male Snowy owl who is reported to have kept two females in nests 1 mi (1·6 km) apart, and a handful of male Great skuas are also known to have been bigamous, their females laying in a single nest. One skua seemed to have a definite preference for two mates because, when one died, another joined so that the triangular relationship lasted for over eight years. Unfortunately no young were reared because two birds would try to incubate at once and eggs were often left exposed to the cold air.

Casual polygyny is often successful because the male helps to feed both families, but the breeding success is lower than in the usual monogamous

111

In the Wilson's phalarope *Steganopus tricolor* of North America, the normal roles of the sexes in courtship are reversed. The female is more brightly coloured and more aggressive than the male and she courts him, chasing away other females. The males alone develop brood patches and incubate the eggs. This sex-reversal is associated with a high level of testosterone, male sex hormone, in female phalaropes and a high level of prolactin, a hormone that controls brood patch development, in males.

families. Several species of wren resort to polygyny quite frequently. The male maintains several nests in one territory and the breeding success is enhanced by the protection given by the domed nest and because, in these species, the female incubates alone and does most of the feeding even when she has the undivided attention of the male. In the European wren, polygyny most frequently occurs where there is plenty of food.

An alternative to the usual pattern of polygyny is a sort of 'reversed polygyny' in which the male cares for the family. The male Mallee fowl builds a nest in which several females lay and tends it himself until the chicks depart. Ostriches are sometimes monogamous but more often a male gathers a small harem into his territory. He mates with each and they lay their eggs in a communal nest. Incubation and care of the young is carried out by the male and the dominant female who drives away the other females.

It is something of a surprise to patriarchal man to find that there are several birds where the female does the courting. She often has the brighter plumage; she aggressively defends the territory, courts the male and lays her eggs in nests which are cared for by him. Each female may mate with several males and leave her eggs scattered among a number of nests. This is cally polyandry. It is rare in man but occurs in mammals where a female will mate with more than one male while on heat.

The Western meadowlark *Sternella neglecta* is a member of the American family Icteridae, not of the true larks. The males establish territories by singing and by ritualized displays but fighting also takes place and deaths occasionally ensue. The ranges of the Western meadowlark and the similar Eastern meadowlark *S. magna* overlap. Males of each species may hold neighbouring territories but interbreeding is avoided by the difference in song. The Eastern meadowlark has a song of two slurred whistles whereas the western species utters seven to ten flute like notes. The female meadowlarks are attracted only to the song of the 'right' males.

A frigatebird or Man-o'-war bird displays its inflatable throat pouch. Frigatebirds nest in trees and bushes. The male selects a suitable place for a nest and advertizes for a mate by inflating its crimson pouch. It also displays by quivering its body with wings outspread. The pouch is deflated when the single egg is laid and the male starts the first stint of incubation. Frigatebirds are related to the gannets and cormorants but, although they live in tropical oceans, they do not swim. Their feathers are not waterproof and they cannot take-off from the sea. On the other hand, they are excellent fliers, having a very large wing area in proportion to their weight.

Only in the birds has the reversal of roles in courtship and parental duties occurred. The habit appears in a variety of birds, apparently where there is an excess of males. It has been recorded occasionally in starlings and habitually in the Painted snipe of the Old World, the tinamous of America, the Pheasant-tailed jaçana, the dotterel, the Red-necked phalarope, the buttonquails, the rheas and probably in the little known Malagasy mesites. Few of these birds have been studied in detail but the female jaçana and Painted snipe are known to hold territories and in the buttonquails, a family of quail-like birds that range from Spain to Australia, the female has a booming call with which she attracts males. When one appears, she courts him, circling around him while booming and stamping the ground. Mating takes place in the normal fashion and the female builds the nest but, when the eggs have been laid, she leaves them to the male and courts another.

The rheas of South America are both polygynous and polyandrous. The males fight each other and court the females which live in small troops. Each male leads several females, one at a time, to his nest and each female will lay in several nests, so both male and female have several mates. The tinamous, guineafowl-like birds of tropical America, have a similar social system.

113

Egg Laying and Nesting

Budgerigars, popular cagebirds but pests in their native Australia, nest in holes. In the wild they chip a cavity in rotten parts of mallee scrub and lay their eggs on a base of wood chips and dust. Captive budgerigars nest freely in nest boxes but, unlike some birds, they need more than courtship and mating to induce egg laying. The female budgerigar will not lay unless she has a nestbox, or is kept in total darkness, and she must be able to hear a male budgerigar. During courtship the male feeds the female, 'bobs' to her and warbles quietly. The warbling is essential for egg formation. It causes the ovaries to develop and the eggs in them to ripen. The speed of development is related to the amount of warbling that the female budgerigar hears.

The stimulus of darkness and warbling act on the ovaries via the nervous system and the endocrine, or hormone producing, glands. Among the birds there are several stimuli important as triggers for egg production. They include the length of day, rainfall, temperature and the availability of food. Ultimately, it is the food supply that matters. Although the breeding season has to be timed so that the eggs hatch when there is sufficient food for feeding the chicks, there must be an abundance of food for the formation of the eggs. Laying down the yolk, albumen and shell for a clutch of eggs, which in small birds may be equal to the total body weight of the female, imposes a strain on her reserves and, as described in the previous chapter, the male often assists by feeding her. Hence, the amount of food available influences the date at which a bird can start laying and also the number of eggs she will lay. Gamebirds lay smaller clutches after hard winters than after mild ones.

Almost all birds lay their eggs in a nest. The few exceptions include the Emperor and King penguins, which balance their eggs on their feet and cover them with a fold of skin; the Fairy tern lays its single egg on a bare branch; nightjars, coursers and sandgrouse lay their eggs on bare ground; birds of prey use the abandoned nests of other birds and the parasites, the cuckoo, cowbirds and others, lay their eggs in other birds' nests. Many reptiles and mammals, and some amphibians and fishes, also make nests. Their function in every instance is to keep the eggs or young together and to protect

Soon after it hatches, the nestling European cuckoo *Cuculus canorus* ejects the eggs of its host, in this case a Tree pipit *Anthus trivialis*. This ensures that the nestling will have the undivided attention of its foster parents. It will grow larger than them and will need all the food they can provide. The young cuckoo usually hatches before the host's eggs and it has a sensitive patch in the middle of its back into which it rolls the eggs. It then braces itself with legs splayed against the nest floor and heaves the eggs over the side. Occasionally some of the other eggs hatch but the nestlings are usually ignored by the parents who concentrate on the larger and stronger cuckoo. If two cuckoo eggs are laid in the same nest, the nestlings try to evict each other for a few days then settle down together.

The Common cormorant *Phalacrocorax carbo* is found in many parts of the world. It builds its nests on rocks or in trees.

them from adverse weather. Nest building in mammals is confined to those species whose young are born helpless and in need of care and protection, but nest-building is necessarily more widespread in birds because they lay eggs which must be kept near body temperature by incubation.

Incubation. A high, even temperature is essential for the proper development of birds' eggs and it is ensured by the behaviour of the parent birds. To maintain the eggs at a temperature only a little lower than that of the incubating parent, they are held against the brood patch, an area on the breast that loses its feathers and develops a rich supply of blood vessels. The presence of a brood patch is a sure sign that a bird has a nest somewhere. Only a few birds, such as cormorants and gannets, do not develop brood patches. They keep their eggs warm with the webs of their feet which are richly supplied with blood vessels. The drive to keep eggs warm is so strong that some birds can be lifted off the nest

and, when released, will return to it despite the potential danger of a nearby human. If an Emperor penguin drops its egg on the snow, every penguin that has not got an egg rushes to pick it up before it freezes. The urge to incubate an egg or, later, to brood a chick becomes so great that the penguins may fight over them. Not only do the eggs and chicks occasionally get crushed in the struggle, the adults get badly cut by their antagonists' bills.

In tropical countries the problem may be to keep the eggs cool. The parent bird stands over the eggs shading them with its wings. The Egyptian plover, one of the coursers, incubates its eggs at night, when the desert air cools rapidly, but during the day it covers them with sand. It will even cool the sand by regurgitating water from its crop. This behaviour has not been studied in detail but it is probable that the Egyptian plover incubates, buries or waters its eggs in such a way that they are kept at a steady temperature throughout the day. Such is the case

115

The cosmopolitan oyster-catcher *Haematopus ostralegus* lays its eggs in a shallow depression in the ground, sometimes lined with pebbles, shells, plants or even rabbit droppings. When disturbed, the sitting adult leaves the nest which, due to the camouflage of the eggs, is very difficult to find. The chicks, too, are extremely well camouflaged.

with the Mallee fowl which lives in the semi-desert mallee scrub country of Australia. The Mallee fowl makes use of solar radiation and vegetable decomposition to provide heat for the developing eggs. The manner in which it does so provides the most complicated example of nesting behaviour in the bird world. The male has sole charge of the nest and it occupies his time for up to 11 months in the year.

In May or June, during the Australian winter, the male Mallee fowl starts to build a large compost heap. He digs a hole up to 4 ft (1·2 m) deep in the sandy soil and dead leaves, scraped together from a radius of 150 ft (45 m), are piled into it. After a soaking by rain, they start to rot and heat is produced, as in a compost heap. Egg laying starts in September and continues for four months. The females seek out a male with a suitable nest and lay their eggs at intervals of two days or more.

The eggs take two months to hatch and, throughout the egg laying and incubation period, the male spends several hours a day ensuring that the nest temperature stays close to 92°F (33°C). The nest, if left to itself, will have a variable temperature because of daily and seasonal changes in the sun's strength and because the speed of rotting changes.

The Mallee fowl smooths out these variations by hard work. He measures the temperature by taking material into his mouth and, if the nest gets too cool, he opens it to let the sun's rays penetrate and spreads out the material to warm in the sun. Then, in the evening, it is piled back onto the eggs to stop them chilling. When the leaves are decomposing rapidly, he may open the nest to let heat out, and, in midsummer, he covers the nest with extra soil to protect it from the fierce sun. Eventually, the chicks hatch, escape from the nest by themselves and run off into the scrub. They are quite independent and the male's work is ended.

Simple and Elaborate Nests. The form that nests take is as varied as the appearance of the birds that make them. They range from simple scrapes in the ground (the Water dikkop lays its eggs on hippopotamus droppings and sandgrouse sometimes lay theirs in large hoofprints) to elaborate structures that show extreme dexterity and perseverance in their construction. Occasionally, nests seem to be unnecessarily elaborate. Nuthatches of the Old World plaster mud and dung round the entrance hole of their nests and the American Red-breasted nuthatch smears the entrance with pine resin, but the Rock nuthatch of the Balkans builds its nest in a rock cleft, and makes a suitable entrance by plastering the opening with a mass of mud and twigs nearly 1,000 times its own weight. This habit may possibly help to reduce predation but the hammerkop or hammerhead, a heavily built African heron, builds a veritable castle for which there seems to be no particular purpose. Unlike the simple platforms that other herons build, the hammerhead's nest is a one-roomed house of mud and sticks, often 6 ft (1·8 m) across, with walls 1 ft (0·3 m) thick and a roof 3 ft (0·9 m) deep. It takes six weeks to build and may even be a disadvantage because other birds and bees like to take it over, sometimes driving the hammerheads away. The South American ovenbird also builds the mud 'house' from which it gets its name and one of its relatives, the White-throated cachalote, builds a domed nest big enough to house a turkey and strong enough for a man to stand on.

Generally, ground-nesting birds make simple nests, often no more than a scrape in the ground scantily lined with grass or pebbles, while those nesting in trees build elaborate affairs in the form of a cup or ball. This is hardly surprising as a tree-nesting bird cannot afford to let its eggs roll out of the nest. A ground-nester, on the other hand, can retrieve its eggs. It stretches out its neck and hooks its bill over the straying egg, so that it nestles under the chin, and draws it towards the body. By nature of its shape, the egg does not roll straight but the bird compensates with movements of the head.

The cup-shaped nests, that are typical of so many birds, appear to be works of art. The materials are delicately woven together in a way that appears impossible with only the use of bill and feet. Most people must have wondered at some time how a nest is built, and, in particular, how it is started; how does the bird anchor the first foundations of its nest to the limbs of a tree or the side of a wall? Certainly, nest building is a laborious job: a pair of swallows was once recorded as making 1,200 trips carrying mud to the nest, and nests of the Long-tailed tit may be lined with over 2,000 small feathers.

An ornithologist once watched North American Wren tits build their cup nests in the forks of branches or among sprays of twigs. He had to be patient as each nest took a week to build. The Wren tits' task is facilitated by the use of sticky spiders' web to bind the material together. First, a

The Black-throated diver *Gavia arctica*. The position of its nest is often marked by a shallow depression where the adults slip down to the water and where the newly-hatched chicks leave the nest shortly after hatching.

hammock of webs is woven between the supporting twigs and is strengthened with more web to form a platform strong enough to take fibres of bark. Bark and web are woven together until about 1 in (25 mm) thick. The Wren tit can then sit on the foundations of its nest and build the walls. Beakfuls of fibre are laid down and bound with web, the loose ends being carefully tucked in. Finally, the interior is lined with more fibres and the exterior decorated with lichen.

The use of sticky spiders' web is a short cut, like using adhesive tape instead of string for wrapping up parcels. Most passerine birds build their cup nests by working the material together, not weaving it as would appear from the finished structure. The bird spins around on the foundations pushing and moulding with its breast and feet so that the material is intertwined and pressed together like felt. Some of the finest nest-builders are, not surprisingly, found in the weaver family, which includes the

buffalo-weavers, the sparrows, the Social weavers and the true weavers. The true weavers, such as the quelea, build nests from strips which they tear off living leaves by grasping an edge in the bill and flying away with it. They prefer the long leaves of grasses and palms, and can destroy crops by defoliating them. The foundation of the nest is composed of a vertical ring of woven leaf strips. Each strip is held with the foot and passed through strips already in place or around the supporting twigs and fastened with a hitch. The next stage is to build on the back of the nest and then to complete the front, so that a tightly woven ball is formed with an entrance hole at the front. The buffalo-weaver builds a nest 3 ft (0·9 m) long and within it he provides a separate nesting chamber for each of his wives, up to six in number. Each chamber has its own entrance to the exterior. Pairs of Social weavers build their nests close together and the Sociable weavers sometimes combine in their

The quetzal or Resplendent trogon *Pharomachrus mocino.* Quetzals nest in tree trunks, excavating their own holes or enlarging old woodpecker holes. The problem of how the male quetzal incubates the eggs without ruining his train was for long a mystery. In Costa Rica it was said to sit facing inwards with the train dangling. In fact, the male quetzal faces the nest hole and the train curves over his back and protrudes through the entrance.

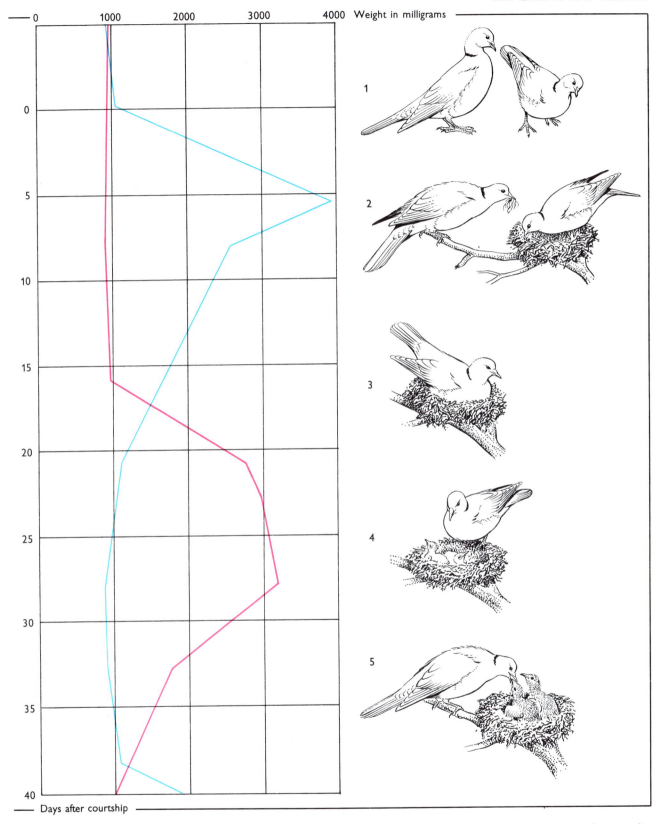

Changes in the weight of the contents of the oviduct (blue) and of the crop (red) in the Ring dove are related to its breeding behaviour. After courtship and mating (1) the eggs in the female begin to grow and reach maturity when nest-building (2) is complete. During incubation (3), normal feeding is resumed and the weight of food in the crop increases, and reaches a maximum just before the young birds hatch (4). This food is then used to feed the young (5).

119

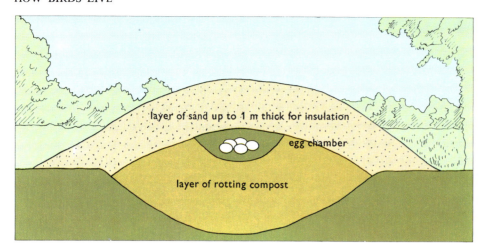

Diagram of the nest of a Mallee fowl. A mass of leaves and other vegetation is scraped into the pit from a wide radius. When the bacterial action of rotting is under way a nest chamber is dug and females arrive to lay their eggs. As many as 35 eggs are laid in one nest, the female laying four times her own weight in eggs over a period of several months. The nest is covered with a thick layer of sand and the male spends the incubation period regulating the temperature to 90°F (33°C) by opening or closing the nest.

layer of sand up to 1 m thick for insulation

egg chamber

layer of rotting compost

hundreds to make what looks like a haystack perched in a tree. Under a communal roof, each pair builds its own nest with a separate entrance.

Nest building is instinctive and it has been found that birds reared in isolation can build nests when provided with suitable material, but their performance will improve with practice. Some details of nest-building may be modifiable by changes in the environment. The American robin builds a separate nest for each of its two broods. It is one of the first birds to lay in the spring and the first nest is made in an evergreen tree. The second is made in deciduous trees which are bare of cover when the

first clutch is laid. The Song sparrow shows similar behaviour. It builds three nests. The first is built under dense herbage at a time when the trees are bare and the next two are placed amongst the foliage. Nests above ground level are generally the safest but they are sitting targets for predators if there are no leaves on the trees.

The hereditary nature of instincts such as nest-building behaviour and the way they can be modified by experience is demonstrated by the effects of hybridising lovebirds. There are six species of lovebird, a small parakeet native to Africa and popular as a cagebird. Four of the species have the strange

The Mallee fowl *Leipoa ocellata* is one of the megapodes or incubator-birds that live in the Indian Ocean, Australasian and Western Pacific regions. The members of this family keep their eggs warm by natural heat instead of sitting on them. Here, the male Mallee fowl is digging a pit in sandy soil which it will fill with leaves. The leaves rot and the heat from their decomposition incubates the eggs. The Brush turkeys and junglefowl also make mounds of vegetation. That of the junglefowl *Megapodius freycinet* may be 35 ft (10.5 m) across and 15 ft (4.5 m) high. Other junglefowl lay their eggs in sandy beaches or in rock crevices which hold their heat at night and, in volcanic areas, the eggs may be warmed by volcanic steam that seeps through the soil.

Nests of the weaver-
birds are made of woven
strips of grass. The male
starts the nest by weav-
ing a vertical ring of
grass secured to suit-
able twigs or stems.
He displays from inside
the ring to attract a
female and mates with
her there. After this, he
completes the nest by
extending the ring back-
wards to form a hemi-
sphere and then adding
the front with the en-
trance hole. Some wea-
vers make long entrance
tubes. That of the Red-
vented weaver is 2 ft
(0.6 m) long. Weavers
use both bill and foot
to work the nest mater-
ial. Each piece is held
down by a foot and the
free end pushed through
strands of the existing
structure, then pulled
through from the other
side and secured with a
knot. The result is a
light but tough con-
struction that protects
the weaver brood from
tropical sun, torrential
rain and predators.

habit of carrying nesting material, which consists of pieces of leaves, by tucking it into their feathers. They ruff up their plumage, tuck the material in, then flatten the feathers to hold it tight. Why they should do this is quite inexplicable, particularly as the other two species carry nest material in the bill, like any other bird. Peach-faced lovebirds, a feather-tucking species, have been crossbred with Masked lovebirds, a bill-carrying species. The offspring were born with a mixture of the two nest material-carrying instincts. They could cut up leaves successfully but did not know how to carry the pieces, although both methods were tried. It took them three years to learn how to carry nest material competently.

Burglar-proof Nests. Important functions of the nest are to deter predators and to hide the eggs from their searching, and many systems of protection have been developed. Nests in holes in trees and in burrows in the ground provide natural protection against all but the lithest of predators and the most severe of weather. Burrowing is particularly common in treeless areas and is found amongst petrels, penguins, puffins, the Burrowing owl and barbets, to name a few. Nests in trees are immune from attacks from earthbound animals but can be robbed by tree-climbers or flying predators and a second line of defence is sometimes employed. The weavers often build their nests near or even under those of bees, wasps, eagles or herons and may nest near human habitation. It seems they gain protec-

tion from the proximity of larger or fiercer animals. The Village weaver nests near the nests of large birds and human dwellings in its native West Africa but associates with wasp nests in Haiti where it has been introduced in the last 300 years. Some tree-nesting weavers and the oropendolas and caciques of America sling their nests from the end of a woven 'rope', as a deterrent to all but the most agile predator. The Red-vented weaver protects its nest by adding an entrance tunnel hanging down from the mouth. It is thought to be a trap for predators because it will come away under the weight of any animal that tries to climb down it to the entrance.

If a nest on the ground is discovered by a predator, there is little that the owners can do, although some of the bolder species attempt to drive or lure the intruder away. The best form of defence is to avoid being discovered in the first place. Where possible, the nest is built under a canopy of vegetation but even on open, cropped swards nests are difficult to find because of the protection afforded by camouflage. If the parent bird is drably coloured, as are female ducks and many waders, it will usually sit tight on the nest until the last possible moment. Brightly marked birds, on the other hand, such as oystercatchers, terns and gulls, fly up while the intruder is still some distance away; sometimes covering the eggs by plants or soil first. These birds rely on the protective colouring of the eggs themselves, usually a green-brown background with irregular dark blotches. The camouflage patterns

◁ The Pied kingfisher *Chloroceryle rudis* of Africa emerges from its nest burrow. To dig the burrow, the kingfishers fly repeatedly at a selected spot, striking it with their bills to dislodge sandy soil. When a depression has been made they cling to the edge and continue to dig. Loose earth is pushed out of the burrow with the tail and feet. There is no lining to the nest chamber but fishbones accumulate around the eggs.

Young Great blue herons *Ardea* ▷ *herodias* standing on their nest. Herons usually nest in trees but sometimes on the ground. The same trees are occupied year after year and some heronries of the Grey heron are known to have been in existence for hundreds of years.

are very effective to human eyes and even to sharp-eyed birds, as was shown by an experiment which showed that crows had greater difficulty finding real gull's eggs than models painted in what to human eyes was a very good imitation.

The value of the camouflage is increased if the predator's attention is not drawn to the possibility of there being any eggs available. Thus, it is an advantage, for the birds, to space their nests so that the predator is only likely to find a nest by accident and, when it does, it will be unlikely to find another by searching. Where birds, such as gulls and terns, do nest in colonies on the ground, this system does not operate. The predator is spurred by a few successes to search the area thoroughly and finds many nests. Its hunting efforts have to be reduced by the parents distracting its attention or by the siting of the colony at a safe place, such as on an island or a cliff.

Cliff and Island Nests. The gulls are mainly ground-nesters, usually choosing such safe nesting sites as islands and marshes, but there has been a tendency among them to nest on cliffs, a nesting habitat that is even more immune from mammalian predators like foxes and weasels. In this habitat they are joined by their close relatives the auks.

Guillemots, for instance, do not make nests but perch in closely-packed rows along cliff ledges. Their eggs are shaped so that they do not roll off the ledges. The egg is longer than is usual and the embryo develops at the sharp end, leaving a large airspace at the blunt end, so that the centre of gravity is at the sharp end and the egg spins in a tight circle. The widespread Herring gull is a ground-nester but some of its very close relatives nest on cliffs. The Glaucous gull will, on occasion, nest on cliffs, while Thayer's gull and the Iceland gull do so regularly. It is noticeable that the latter two make deeper nests than does the Herring gull and that the eggs of the Thayer's gull are often shaped like those of guillemots. Another important adaptation is that when disturbed, the chicks of these species 'freeze' rather than run to shelter – a vital reaction on a cliff ledge. The kittiwake nests on minute ledges, often with just enough room for the pair to stand. Its behaviour is basically that of a gull, but several aspects have been adapted to prevent falling off. The nest is a deep cup of mud, a material not used by other gulls, the chicks do not move and have strong claws and toes for gripping and the female squats rather than stands during mating.

Pallas' fishing eagle *Haliaetus leucoryphus* of central Asia at its nest of twigs. Eagles may have more than one nest in their territories. They are used repeatedly with new material being added at the start of each breeding season.

A nuthatch *Sitta europaea* delivers a beak-full of insects to its young. Nuthatches have the strong claws characteristic of other tree climbers, such as the woodpeckers and tree-creepers, but, unlike these, nuthatches do not use the tail as a prop and can descend tree trunks headfirst. All but two species of nuthatch nest in holes in trees, or in nestboxes. Many plaster the entrance to the nest with mud and dung, and in one case pine resin. This is presumed to deter competitors for the nest site. However, a nuthatch will also plaster the narrow cracks in a nestbox. The Rock nuthatch lives in the rocky hills of South-west Asia and walls up a rock crevice to make a neat apartment.

Islands form another refuge from ground predators. Apart from the obvious use of ready made islands, several birds make their own. Swans, grebes, coots and other rails nest on large piles of water plants that they gather together. If the water level rises, more material is added to keep the eggs dry with the result that, after a flood has dropped, the eggs may be perched well above the water. The nests of grebes and the Giant coot sometimes float free and the jaçanas may lay their eggs on a water-lily leaf or on a nest of a few rush stems. The Horned coots of high Andean lakes are the heavy engineers of the bird world. Their nests are built on small islets, usually using natural ones but on one lake they construct their own out of stones. The coots collect the stones in their bills from the shore or lake bed and pile them into heaps 6 ft (1·8 m) high and 13 ft (4 m) in diameter.

Forced Fostering. There can be few people living in Europe who do not know that the cuckoo lays its eggs in the nests of other birds and that the cuckoo chick ejects its nest mates so that its foster parents give it their sole attention. Not all members of the cuckoo family behave in this way. The American cuckoos rear their own young and the American counterpart of the European cuckoo is the cowbird of the American oriole family. Other parasites are the whydahs or widow-birds, the honeyguides, the Black-headed duck of South America, the Red-crested pochard of eastern Europe and the Parasitic weaver. Brood parasitism, as this behaviour is known, is remarkable in its occurrence but the more it is investigated the more incredible is it found to be in its details. The para-

sites have evolved complex mechanisms to ensure that their eggs go into the right nests and are not rejected by the hosts. The female European cuckoo keeps watch at the nests of small birds and slips in to lay an egg while the owner is away and before the clutch is complete. The Brown-headed cowbird, the most parasitic of the cowbirds, behaves similarly but the Indian koel is said to resort to a ruse to lure the hosts away. The male koel is black. It flies towards a crow's nest and is chased off by the crows who mistake it for another crow trespassing on their territory. Meanwhile the brown female koel slips in to lay her egg.

After laying, the European cuckoo swallows or throws out one of the host's eggs, as does the cowbird. In both, the parasite eggs hatch after a shorter incubation period than is needed by the host eggs. The young parasite chick is thereby given a head start over its nest mates. The young cuckoo uses this time to eject all the eggs or nestlings so that it is alone in the nest. Cowbirds lack this behaviour and the host rears some of its own offspring alongside the parasite, although they may be starved out by the larger, voracious cowbird chick. The honeyguides parasitize mainly barbets, woodpeckers and other hole-nesting birds. Their chicks use a sharp hook on each half of the bill for killing their nest mates.

A major problem facing brood parasites is that the hosts react to unfamiliar objects in the nest and feed only those nestlings that present the correct signals. Faced with a strange egg the host may eject it or desert the nest completely. Tyrant flycatchers even build a false floor over offending

◁ A Yellow-eyed babbler *Chrysomma sinense* fits neatly into its nest which is built near the ground. Some are open cups while others have domed roofs. The materials for the nest are fronds of moss and bark fibres which are neatly held in place with spiders' webs.

Mute swans *Cygnus olor* at their ▷ nest. The nest is a large heap of reeds, rushes or other vegetation, and may be surrounded by shallow water or built on dry land. The male (cob) gathers the material while the female (pen) fashions it into a nest.

A European swallow *Hirundo rustica* at its cup-shaped nest. The foundation of the nest is made by plastering mud to a wall where a slight irregularity provides the initial support.

cowbird eggs. The problem is overcome by the parasites ability to mimick the patterns of the host's eggs. This is not a simple matter for the European cuckoo, as it parasitizes over 180 species or for the Brown-headed cowbird which uses the nests of over 250 species. The mechanism of egg mimicry has been well studied in the European cuckoo. Examination of parasitized nests shows that the cuckoo's egg is nearly always remarkably similar to those of the host. In a particular locality the cuckoos will have a favoured host and their eggs have evolved to mimic the eggs of this host. In Hungary, cuckoo eggs mimic those of the Great reed warbler, in Finland they mimic the red-start and whinchat. A mismatch occurs when the cuckoo cannot find a nest of its preferred host and has to utilize another species. This happens more often than not in England where there is a very high rate of mismatches. English cuckoos lay mainly in the nests of dunnocks, Reed warblers and Meadow pipits but also in a wide range of others. Surprisingly, its eggs are very unlike those of the dunnock, a major host. The explanation appears to be that, over Europe, each locality has a race of cuckoos adapted to a specific host, but in England, there is such a variety of habitats with a consequent wide variety of host species in a small area, none of which nest in large numbers, that a race of cuckoos specializing in one host cannot evolve. Egg mimicry is absent in cowbirds, while in the honeyguides and widow-birds the situation is simple because both the host and parasite eggs are pure white.

The problem of ensuring that the parasite chick is fed by the host is solved in two ways: ejection or killing of nest mates and mimicking them. The cowbirds do neither but they survive by hatching first

Nests of Village weavers or Black-headed weavers *Ploceus cucullatus* in an Acacia tree. The nests are suspended from slender twigs and the birds enter through hanging entrance tubes. Colonies of this species are often found in association with other species. This happens when the species have chosen the same safe site. Such a site may occur over water, where predators cannot reach, near the nests of birds of prey or wasps, or by human dwellings.

and so become bigger and stronger than their hosts. The chicks of the koel look like baby crows and are fed with them but the widow-birds have evolved a mimicry equivalent in detail to the egg mimicry of the European cuckoo. They parasitize waxbills of the family Estrildidae but do not destroy any of the host's eggs, so that the host later feeds predigested seeds to both its own chicks and that of the widow-bird. It puts its beak into the gape of the nestling and pumps in the food, a method unique among the passerine birds. The signal for feeding is a complex pattern of black spots and white or blue papillae in the mouth of the nestling. Each species of waxbill has its own gape pattern and the parasitic widow-bird nestling must imitate the pattern if it is to be fed. Thus it is essential for the female widow-bird to lay her egg in the nest of the right species of waxbill. The Paradise widow-bird

occurs in seven races, each of which parasitizes a different waxbill species. For the purity of the races to be maintained the females must mate with males of the same race. This is facilitated by the male widow-bird mimicking the song of the waxbill in whose nest it was reared.

There are still many unsolved problems concerning the relations between brood parasites and their hosts and the most basic is how brood parasitism arose. It has been suggested that the habit arose through birds laying their eggs in the wrong nest. An indication is seen in some North American cuckoos which usually build their own nests but sometimes lay their eggs in the nest of a pair of their own species. Others occasionally lay eggs in the nest of a different species but these fail to hatch; they have not yet evolved the necessary characteristics for successful parasitism.

An Indian courser *Cursorius coromandelicus* with its two eggs. The eggs are well camouflaged and are laid on bare ground so that they are very difficult to see. Coursers live in hot parts of the Old World and the eggs have to be shaded from the sun rather than incubated. The Egyptian plover, a courser not a plover, incubates its egg during the cool of the night and covers them with sand during the day. It may even bring water to moisten the sand and cool it.

Raising the Family

At the end of the period of incubation the chick is ready to emerge from the egg. From a small disc of cells, the embryo has developed into an infant bird that, neatly packed, fills the entire space within the eggshell. The protective layer of egg white or albumin is absorbed, the remains of the yolk are stored in the body to provide a food supply during the first few days after hatching, and the thickness of the eggshell has been reduced. The calcium in the shell has been used to build bones in the chick's body and the consequent weakening of the shell makes hatching easier. The heart will have been beating for some time but, two or three days before hatching, the chick comes alive. It changes its position so that its bill penetrates the air space at the blunt end of the egg and it starts to breathe. Many chicks begin to call at the same time with a thin but easily heard voice, known as peeping.

The chick is now ready to force its way out of the eggshell but its life has already begun. Its peeping acts as a signal to the other chicks in the nest and to its parent, and a series of behavioural patterns, initiated by instinct and guided by learning, are set under way to lead the chick through the hazards of early life and to leave it able to find its own food and guard against attack. The process of growing up involves both parents and chick. The parents are needed to feed, protect and care for the growing chick, a role that varies considerably between species. It is absent in the Mallee fowl, where the chick fights its way out of the nest mound and runs off alone into the scrub. It never sees its parents and is independent from the start, being able to fly within 24 hours of hatching. At the other extreme, young birds of prey are dependent on their parents for several months after they have fledged.

The emergence of a brood of ostriches. In the top picture the eggs are being incubated by the female ostrich. She may be sitting on as many as 60 eggs, the clutches of several females laid in one nest. Ostriches are unusual in that the young chicks do not have the egg tooth that other birds use for knocking holes in the eggshell. They share this feature with the Incubator birds; in both the young are very well developed at hatching and are strong enough to force their way out by movements of the body. When the chick emerges it is damp from the egg fluids, and the remains of the allantois, the membrane through which it breathed as an embryo, are still attached. Although the lungs start to work as soon as the bill penetrates the airspace, they cannot supply the bird with sufficient oxygen until the eggshell is opened. Thus, the allantois has to function until the moment of hatching. Within a few hours the ostrich chicks have dried out and are active. They can follow their parents and, when only a month old, can run as fast as them.

130

Active and Helpless Young. The chick's first job in life is to break its way out of the eggshell. This is done without any assistance from the parents, except in a few cases, but it is aided by two things. The eggshell has been weakened by the transference of calcium to the growing chick, and the tip of the chick's bill is reinforced by a horny lump called the egg tooth. The egg tooth drops off when the chick is a few days old and its sole function is to help knock holes in the eggshell, a process called pipping, that is aided by a strong muscle in the neck. As soon as the bill has punctured the shell, the chick moves slightly and makes another hole next to the first. It continues this manoeuvre until there is a ring of holes, or a continuous split, around the shell near the broadest part. Eventually the blunt end of the shell comes away and the chick forces its way out.

Emergence from the eggshell takes from several hours in the small birds to three or four days in curlews, albatrosses and others. The chick is quite helpless at first. Its head flops on the floor of the nest and its coat of down is plastered against its body by the egg fluids. The parents have to defend it against predators and keep it warm by brooding. While the chick is very young brooding is continuous. It nestles against the brood patch in the same way as the egg is incubated. When the down has dried and formed a fluffy layer, the chick can be left unattended for varied periods, depending on the weather, but the chicks of songbirds and others are born naked and brooding must be continued for many days.

The degree of helplessness in a newly hatched chick falls into two distinct types. The young Mallee fowl is quite exceptional, but the chicks of many species leave the nest when only a few hours old. They are known as precocial birds. When hatched they have a dense coat of down, their eyes are open and their other senses alert. The legs are strong and the chicks are soon running about in search of food. An alternative name for them is nidifugous or nest-leaving young. Nidifugous young are found among the ground-nesting birds such as gamebirds, waders, ducks and grebes. It is likely that nidifugy

The embryo of a chicken at a late stage of development. It is fully formed and the down covering the body can be seen clearly. In front of the head is the yellow yolk sac with the network of bloodvessels that transport the food from the yolk to the embryo.

◁ The fulmar *Fulmaris glacialis* usually nests on cliff ledges but in some places it has taken to nesting at the base of stone dykes or inside ruined houses. Fulmars deter intruders by spitting an evil smelling oil, as this one is doing. They start by gaping at the intruder, then retching convulsively until a stream of oil is produced. The oil is secreted from the lining of the proventriculus, the front part of the stomach.

The Tree pipit *Anthus trivialis,* ▷ like all pipits, nests on the ground and feeds its young on insects. Although a ground nester, the Tree pipit requires trees or even fence posts as singing posts before it can colonize an area. A relative lives on the Antarctic island of South Georgia where its nests may be found by those of the giant Wandering albatross.

is the primitive form of childhhod in birds because young reptiles, the ancestors of birds, hatch in an advanced state of development and immediately fend for themselves. The chicks, or nestlings, of the second type are markedly different. They hatch out naked, blind and helpless. They spend a considerable time in the nest and are virtually spoon fed by the parents. These birds are altricial or nidicolous, that is, nest dwellers. They include the songbirds, birds of prey, parrots, pigeons and hole-nesters such as woodpeckers, hornbills and king-fishers.

The eggs of nidicolous species have a shorter period of incubation than those of nidifugous species. As a result, the chicks are less advanced in all respects except in their digestive systems. All they can do at first is weakly raise their heads and open their bills for their parents to fill with food. The nervous system is relatively undeveloped except for a few reflexes. The most important of these can be tested at any songbird's nest where the young still have their eyes shut. A tap on the side of the nest, simulating the arrival of the parent with food, causes the chicks to raise their heads and 'gape', presenting widely opened bills. After the eyes have opened the reflex wanes and the chicks direct their gaping towards the parent. The gape is an important stimulus to the parent bird to feed the chicks and most nidicolous chicks have brightly coloured mouths to attract the attention of the

parents. The nestlings of the Estrildidae, an Old World family that includes the waxbills, mannikins, avadavat and many other popular cagebirds, have conspicuous patterns of spots and papillae in the mouth. Each species has its peculiar pattern and the parents only put food, predigested seeds, into mouths having the right pattern. In Africa some of the waxbills are parasitized by widow-birds, whose nestlings must, as we have seen, have the same mouth pattern as their nest mates if they are to be fed.

The Family Bond. In his well-known book *King Solomon's Ring*, Konrad Lorenz describes how he became foster-mother to a brood of goslings. He found that if newly hatched goslings saw him before they saw their mother they would follow him rather than her. Detailed observations showed that goslings learn the characteristics of their parent very rapidly and, once learnt, they are never forgotten. This phenomenon is called imprinting. In natural conditions goslings, as well as ducklings, young moorhens and many others, imprint on their mothers but, in artificial conditions, they can be led to imprint on humans, model birds, wooden boxes and any variety of objects. There is a very obvious value of this behaviour to a young bird that has to leave the nest and follow a parent within a day or so of birth: the family keeps together from the start and the parent can easily lead them to food and safety.

Recognition of the parents by the young, or *vice versa*, is not needed to such an extent among nidicolous species, or in nidifugous species where the young stay within a territory that is not occupied by young of other broods. If the young stay in the nest it is sufficient for the parents to recognize the position of the nest. Recognition is, however, necessary where the parent has to pick out its offspring among hundreds or thousands of chicks in a dense colony. Some terns call as they arrive at the colony with food for their chicks; the chicks, waiting near the nest, or, in Royal terns, grouped in crèches, respond only to the voices of their own parents who then fly down to them.

Among the albatrosses, there is a variety of recognition behaviour related to the nesting habit. Black-browed and Grey-headed albatrosses nest in dense colonies on cliff tops. The nests are packed together and the sitting birds are just out of range of each other. The chicks of these two albatrosses stay on the nest until it is time to fly. In fact, if they fall off

accidentally they cannot climb back onto the tall cylinder of mud that comprises the nest. The adults of these species recognize only the nest and will feed any chick that is placed on their nest. The Wandering albatross nests on flat ground or on ridges. The nests are well scattered and chicks often leave their nests, particularly near fledging time. The adults recognize their own chicks and will search for them if they find the nest empty.

In these two types of nesting habit, the parent albatross are equipped with the behaviour needed to find their young. In the northern part of the family's range, the Waved albatross of the Galapagos has a nesting habit that resembles that of many penguins. The young albatrosses leave their nests and gather in small crèches under bushes. As with penguins, parents returning with food must pick out their own offspring from the mob. Their task is made easier by the chicks also being able to recognize their parents and coming forward to be fed.

133

A remarkable finding is that the formation of a bond between parents and offspring may start before the egg hatches, when the chick starts to peep. For two days before the brood hatches a mallard duck holds a two-way conversation with her ducklings. She clucks quietly and they respond with peeping. During this period it seems that the ducklings learn their mother's voice and consequently imprint on her more readily when they hatch. Between 16 and 32 hours after hatching the duck leads her brood from the nest, calling as she goes. It is essential that the ducklings are fully imprinted by this time or they will be left in the nest to starve. This raises a second point about peeping. All the ducklings in a brood have to be of the same age, otherwise the youngest are in danger of being left behind. They have to hatch out at the same time, although there will have been a considerable difference in the time the laying of the first and last eggs in a large clutch, up to 16 in the mallard. It might be expected that this difference would be repeated

in the hatching times, but a clutch of mallard eggs hatches during a period of 3 to 8 hours. To some extent synchronized hatching is effected by the eggs not being incubated until the last is laid, but warm weather and the necessity for the duck to sit on the nest when laying means that development of the first eggs before the last is laid cannot be prevented. Ultimately, synchrony is effected by the ducklings hearing each other peeping. How this works is not known, perhaps the ducklings are responding to the duck's calls, but synchronous hatching occurs in many precocial birds where it is essential for the brood to leave the nest *en masse*. The dozen eggs in the clutch of the Greater prairie chicken, a grouse of eastern North America, hatch within the space of an hour.

Among altricial birds, synchronous hatching is not so important, as the chicks stay in the nest and some benefit is gained from a staggered hatching. Incubation starts with the first egg and the eggs hatch at the same intervals of time as they were

A male Reed bunting *Emberiza schoeniclus* feeds its nestlings. The nesting season is an unusually busy time for some male Reed buntings. There are often two broods raised each year and the buntings may change their mates during the course of the breeding season.

A Great crested grebe *Podiceps cristatus* on its nest of reeds. The eggs hatch at two-day intervals and the older chicks nestle on the parents' back, away from the waterlogged nest. When all the chicks have emerged the parents carry the chicks as they search for food. Later, the chicks take to the water and follow their parents.

laid. As a result the oldest chick is noticeably larger than the youngest. When the parent returns to the nest with food the larger chicks push their younger siblings to one side and claim the meal. Only when they are replete do they stop thrusting forward and allow the smaller ones to be fed. In times of plenty, all members of the brood are properly fed. They beg for and receive food in rotation but, if food is scarce, the older chicks will be continually scrambling for food and the youngsters go hungry. As they become weaker their chances of being fed diminish, until they die.

Nature appears to be cruel, but a system of staggered hatching ensures that as many healthy chicks can be reared as the food supply allows. In Barn owls there is a two day gap between the laying and consequent hatching of the eggs. The oldest chick may hatch a fortnight before the youngest, so then the younger members of the brood are at a clear disadvantage. The food of Barn owls is mainly small rodents, whose numbers vary enormously from year to year. In times of abundance, a pair of Barn owls can catch sufficient prey to feed all their chicks but in famine years many of them will die. But the youngest die to save one or two of the eldest chicks. All the food is taken by the largest and strongest and the owl pair produces a few healthy chicks, with a good expectancy of survival, instead of half a dozen doomed weaklings. A similar pattern is seen in the Great skua of the Antarctic. Its two eggs hatch two days apart and in the blizzard conditions that occur even in summer it may have difficulty foraging. The chicks get very hungry and the elder chick may drive the younger out of the territory or even kill and eat it.

Keeping the Nest Clean. Among the first duties of a parent bird is that of keeping the nest clean. It is a duty that can be neglected by nidifugous birds who lead their chicks from the nest at an early age, never to return, but where the chicks stay in the nest until they fledge, it is a continuous chore. The nest must be kept clean of droppings, dead chicks, stale food and, initially, of broken eggshells. Broken eggshells are removed by many nidicolous birds but the removal of droppings by the parents is a habit found mainly in the passerines; in other

135

birds the chicks usually defaecate over the side of the nest. Keeping the nest clean serves two functions, sanitation and protection. Removal of remains of food, dead chicks and, most important, the droppings reduces the risk of infection and prevents the down of the chicks becoming wet and matted, so losing its insulating capacity. The young of many birds, including many sea birds and birds of prey, squirt their droppings over the side of the nest, as do the sitting adults. The nest soon becomes ringed with white and the system is seen to be less than perfect in packed colonies of penguins, gannets or albatrosses where the chicks keep their own nests clean but foul their neighbours with a strong, odorous jet.

The passerines usually nest in deep cup-shaped nests and they have evolved a method of extruding droppings in a membraneous sac. The nestling turns and presents its cloaca to the parent who picks up the sac as it is ejected. When the nestlings are very young, parents swallow the sacs but later they are carried away and dropped. The female lyrebird goes so far as to dunk the sac in a nearby stream or to bury it.

Carrying the droppings from the vicinity of the nest has the added advantage of preventing the nest from being made conspicuous by a splash of white, but droppings are often removed from nests hidden in holes or burrows. Woodpeckers remove droppings in sacs but the burrows of kingfishers become fouled. However, the young kingfishers protect their growing feathers in waxy sheaths until they emerge from the nest.

The remains of the eggshells present another problem, for it is possible for the young chicks to be injured or smothered by eggshells. Many birds, again excepting nidifugous species, carry away or swallow the eggshells. Eggshells lying in or around the nest are a lure for predators; the exterior is well camouflaged but the interior is often shiny white. This is an extra reason for carrying them well away from the nest. For the Black-headed gull which breeds in colonies with nests only a yard or so apart, removing eggshells can be dangerous in itself. The newly hatched chick is very vulnerable and, if the parent leaves the nest, the chick runs the danger of being eaten by a neighbouring gull. Consequently, eggshell removal is delayed for a few hours until the chick has dried out, becoming fluffy and hard to swallow.

Defending the Family. Throughout its life a bird has to be on its guard against danger but its life is most seriously threatened when it is young and unable to fly, unless it is of a species that is fortunate enough to nest on an uninhabited island or other secure place. The young bird's safety depends on keeping out of a predator's way or on active defence by the parents. Hole-nesting species have a natural immunity to most predators and wrynecks and tits reinforce this by imitating the hiss of a snake when disturbed on the nest. Other birds rely on camouflage to escape the notice of predators. The chicks of ground-living birds in particular, make use of blotched patterns on their down to render themselves difficult to detect, witness the difficulty of finding chicks in a tern colony when they crouch motionless among pebbles and scattered vegetation. Camouflage is of little use unless the chick keeps still because predators are quick to detect movement and many birds have alarm calls that cause their chicks to squat motionless or run to cover. Incidentally, chicks of the turnstone may 'freeze' while still in the egg, another example of early communication between parent and young.

A second line of defence involves the more active participation of the parent birds. They seek to turn the attention of the predator towards themselves and away from the brood. A continuous warning call and conspicuous flutter may serve this purpose, but many birds that nest in open country have special displays for luring predators. In the simplest form the parent bird flops on the ground, beating its wings. A Meadow pipit usually flies explosively off its nest when disturbed but sometimes it will land and flutter a few yards from the nest, then fly a little farther and flutter away. A predator is attracted to this activity until the pipit finally flies away, leaving the predator with little chance of finding its way back to the well concealed nest.

The waders have developed two forms of specialized luring behaviour, known as distraction displays. Both serve to make the bird conspicuous. In the so-called broken-wing display, the bird lets one wing hang limp as if injured. Whether Nature has, as it were, designed the posture to make the predator think the bird really is injured is debatable and perhaps far-fetched, although to human eyes

The fieldfare *Turdus pilaris*, a large thrush, feeds its ▷ nestlings with earthworms. The orange mouths act as a marker signal, stimulating the adult to fill them with food. As each nestling becomes replete, it stops gaping and the adults concentrate on feeding the others.

The Black drongo or King crow *Dicrurus macrocercus* fiercely attacks any bird of prey or crow that comes near its nest. Small birds are left alone and they may nest in the same tree as the drongo and so be protected from predators. The drongo's aggressiveness does not protect it from the Indian Drongo cuckoo which lays its eggs in drongos' nests. It avoids being attacked by resembling the drongo in having both black plumage and a forked tail.

it is a good piece of acting. What is very noticeable is that the drooping wing uncovers a flash of white plumage and that the displaying bird runs across the line of vision so as to make it conspicuous. The second form of distraction display, the so-called rodent-run, also shows off conspicuous plumage. The bird is said to be imitating the movement of a small mammal, but it is difficult to see why a bird should trouble to imitate a mammal to attract a predator such as a fox that hunts birds. In the rodent-run, the bird runs with arched back, tail depressed and sometimes flutters its wings. The fluttering may give an impression of a scurrying mouse but it also serves to draw attention to the bird. The posture also displays the white flashes at the base of the tail of two species that regularly perform the rodent-run – the Ringed plover and Purple sandpiper. The display is orientated so that the bird runs directly away from the predator, so showing the white flashes to the best advantage.

Whatever may be the derivation of distraction displays, and this may be unanswerable, they are

certainly effective. There is one record of a North American Long-billed curlew that lured a coyote from its nest. When last seen, the two were disappearing over a hill, half a mile away.

While performing a distraction display a bird is playing safe. It keeps out of reach of the predator and, if the predator is a mammal, it can always fly to safety. A more dangerous form of defence is to attack, not so much with the intention of injuring a predator but of confusing it. A small bird attacking a flesh-eating bird or mammal in defence of its brood can be said to be behaving altruistically. It runs a real risk of being caught itself, which, for the survival of the species, is a bad thing. It is better for the parents to let the brood die and live to lay again. Not surprisingly, then, active defence is rare and only few birds are well known for their aggressive behaviour.

The birds of prey and owls are only occasionally dangerous during the breeding season but swans and geese are to be treated with caution. The drongos of the Old World tropics are famous for their fearless defence of the nest and in Zaire (Congo), one drongo is called the 'angry leopard'. Drongos attack hawks, owls, crows, hornbills and snakes but they do not molest small birds, which will nest near a drongo's nest for the protection it affords. The skuas are also famous for their aggression towards intruders coming near their nests. Uttering hoarse cries, they swoop at the intruder, sweeping past his head and sometimes hitting him with the feet or wing tips. The attacks become more violent as the intruder nears the nest or chicks and the skuas may even land on a man's shoulders to peck at him. Wherever the Great skua breeds, in Iceland, northern Britain, the Falkland Islands or the Antarctic, it is often regarded as a pest. Work in a skua's territory becomes difficult and sheep, dogs and horses are harried. The skuas seem to react aggressively to any large animal which could harm their offspring and even Fur seals on sub-Antarctic islands are pestered by skuas and sent running.

Skuas belong to the same family as the gulls and terns, many of which also attack trespassers. They are not so violent as the skuas but the members of a colony often attack in a concerted effort. To anyone not used to them, the first visit to a tern colony can be quite alarming. Like dive-bombers,

the terns drop vertically at the intruder, then climb sharply having delivered an ear-splitting shriek just by his head. Black-headed gulls suit their style of defence to the nature of the predator. A falcon that hunts only adult birds inspires fear and the gulls flee from it. Crows and hedgehogs which feed only on eggs or chicks elicit violent attacks from the parent gulls but foxes, and man, which prey on both adults and brood are treated with a mixture of aggression and fear. The gulls swoop at them, then soar away, in the same pattern as already described for the skuas and terns. The urge to drive such predators from the colony is balanced by a care not to get too near them.

Feeding the Family. Sanitation and defence are incidental to the main task of parent birds which is to supply their offspring with food until they can fend for themselves. For nidifugous birds this task is minimal. The chicks leave the nest and are able to gather their own food within a few hours of hatching. The role of the parent in this context is limited to showing where food can be found. The domestic chicken, for instance, calls to her brood when she has found food but the chicks have to pick it up for themselves and learn to distinguish edible from inedible objects. Among nidicolous species, the young have to be fed in the nest and some

A coot *Fulica atra* with young. The young coots have brightly coloured heads which probably serve to direct the parents when presenting food, as do the bright gapes of passerine nestlings. The brood stays with the parents for one month, returning to the nest at night. At first the parents do not recognize their own chicks and will feed any chick of about the right size. After a fortnight they become more discerning and attack strange chicks. At the same time, the chicks only solicit from their own parents. Coots raise two or three broods a year and chicks of the first brood will help to feed younger chicks.

birds continue to feed fledged young until they have learned the skills needed for hunting.

The parents' task is to give the chicks as much food as they can take so that they grow rapidly and become independent as soon as possible. The fledging period is a time of physiological strain for the parents, for they must search for extra food, and there may be only a short period when food is sufficiently abundant for the chicks to be fed properly. The importance of this is not so obvious in temperate regions where there is a period of relative abundance throughout the summer months, but it is very clear in hot, dry countries where birds have to raise their young on a flush of seeds or insects that becomes available after a short rainy season. In desert regions a single rainstorm can initiate nesting in a limited area. Nevertheless, the timing of breeding in temperate regions is often geared so that hatching coincides with a particular abundance of food. The European robin feeds its young mainly on leaf-eating caterpillars. It lays, and hatches, its eggs some weeks before the Spotted flycatcher which feeds its young on the flying adult insects.

Among the garden and woodland birds of temperate regions the abundant food supply often lasts long enough for two or three broods to be reared, particularly if it becomes abundant early in the year. The pigeons can continue nesting longer than other birds because they feed their young on 'pigeons' milk'. A remarkable parallel to the milk of mammals, pigeon's milk is secreted from the lining of the crop of adult pigeons during the nestling period. It looks and smells rather like cheese and contains 13–18 per cent protein and 7–13 per cent fat. It is rich in vitamins but lacks calcium. For the first few days, the nestlings are fed on nothing but milk, but afterwards the milk is supplemented with the adults' food. The milk ensures that fast-growing young have a rich supply of protein, which is deficient in grain and leaves, the usual food of pigeons. Many other seed-eating birds, such as the weavers and sparrows, give their young the extra protein they need for growth by feeding them insects.

Most nestlings do not need to drink. They get sufficient liquid from their food. A few, the European cormorant for example, bring water to the chicks in the crop but sandgrouse bring water to the nest by soaking the breast feathers. Sandgrouse live in the deserts and plains of Asia, Africa and eastern Europe. They live on a diet of dry seeds and have to drink regularly. Their distribution is consequently restricted to about a 50 mile (80 km) radius from water and they make regular daily flights to water holes and rivers. The chicks, too, are fed on seeds and need water, which is brought to them in the breast feathers of the male. The barbules of the breast feathers lack hooks and lie coiled along the barbs. When soaked they uncoil and trap water by surface tension. A male sandgrouse can carry up to 40 ml of water in its feathers. About half will be lost by evaporation as it flies back to the nest but sufficient remains for the chicks' thirst to be quenched.

Prolonged Childhood. For many birds the parental duties cease when the young leave the nest or even before. Members of the petrel family feed their chicks so well that they may become heavier than their parents. They are then abandoned and left on the nest until ready to fly. The chicks of shearwaters become so fat that they are taken in large

Male sandgrouse are able to bring water to their chicks by soaking their own breast feathers when they drink. When they return to the nest, the chicks drink by running the wet feathers between their bills.

The chicks of the King penguin *Aptenodytes patagonica* gather in a huge group called a crèche while their parents go fishing. On returning, an adult penguin will pick out its own chick and refuses to feed other chicks that solicit food from it.

numbers in many parts of the world, from the Canaries and Tristan da Cunha to Australia and New Zealand, where they are called muttonbirds.

Abandoning the young in the nest is probably the exception rather than the rule. Many songbirds continue to feed their fledglings for several days. An unfortunate consequence of the nestlings being left on low branches or even on the ground while their parents forage is that people assume that they have been abandoned, particularly as the fledglings are slow to fly, and 'rescue' them.

When the fledglings are eventually abandoned and left to their own resources, the parents are free to raise another brood, but some birds appear to manage to squeeze two broods into a short season by overlapping. The sugarbirds, long-billed nectar-drinkers of South Africa, feed their young for three weeks after they have fledged, by which time they will have started to incubate the second brood. Presumably the abundance of nectar, as well as insects and spiders, on the *Protea* bushes in which they live, is ample enough to make this possible. Among the coots and moorhens, the position is reversed. The young stay with their parents but are capable of fending for themselves and even help to feed the second brood and raise the level of the nest in times of flood.

Parental care after fledging is needed where the fledglings have to be kept alive and in good health while they learn to feed themselves. It is a trait that is best developed in hunting birds where considerable skill is needed to catch food. Even among adults the failure rate of hunting may be quite high and, as the parents do not teach the young, hunting must be learnt by experience. Young owls, hawks and eagles spend a few weeks or months in their parents' territories before moving away. The young of the African crowned eagle are fed for about 10 months after they have fledged and the species can breed only once in every two years. The frigatebird of tropical seas is also limited in its breeding rate. This bird has a specialized way of life. It feeds by stealing from other birds and by catching fish, particularly flying fish, at the surface of the sea. Although related to the gannets its plumage is not waterproof and it cannot land on the sea, so the

The gaping mouths of the young is such an attraction to the parent cardinal *Pyrrhuloxia cardinalis,* that they have even been known to put food in the open mouth of a goldfish.

fish are picked up from the air. Not only do the chicks take five or six months to fledge, they are fed by their parents for a further two to six months while they learn the techniques of precision hunting.

Life for the parent frigatebird and Crowned eagle is made easier by the relative abundance of food all the year round, but in the southern polar regions the larger species of albatross and penguin face the problem of a very short summer season followed by many months of extremely adverse weather in winter. The two great albatrosses, the Wandering and the Royal albatross, cannot bring off their single chicks in one summer season. Their solution has been to leave the chick on the nest for the winter. It receives food at intervals until the next summer, when it grows its feathers and leaves the nest. By then it is too late for the parents to lay again and they leave the colony until the following year. The King penguin, twice the size of most other penguins, behaves in the same manner as the great albatrosses, whose island homes it shares. The chicks are not fed very frequently during the winter and lose weight. If they start the winter at too low a weight, they die before the spring. If they

The skylark *Alauda arvensis* is famous for its prolonged warbling song and has been introduced to Canada, Australia, New Zealand and Hawaii. Like all larks it nests on the ground but it lives in damper situations than most species. The nest is very well camouflaged and difficult to find unless the bird is flushed. In some desert larks a small wall of pebbles is built around one side of the nest, presumably as a protection against the wind. The camouflage of the nest is aided in the desert-living larks by the back feathers of the adult matching the colour of the ground. In one part of Arabia, a dark form of the Desert lark lives on black larva and a pale sandy form lives on sand.

survive the winter, they rapidly put on weight and go to sea around midsummer.

It is a matter of some interest that the great albatrosses and the King penguin have found the same solution to a common problem but it is more noteworthy that the King penguin's closest relative, the Emperor penguin, has found a radically different solution to a more intense form of the same problem. The Emperor penguin breeds on the Antarctic continent, hundreds of miles farther south than does the King penguin, where the weather is worse and the sun does not rise during the winter. It sends its chick into the world during the short summer period of ease and abundance by laying its egg in midwinter. The chick emerges in July or August and by January is ready to fend for itself although it does not achieve the full adult weight until the following year.

Winter Retreats

The Dark Ages that descended on Europe as the Roman Empire collapsed resulted in a severe setback in learning. Historians now suggest that these times were not as dark as was once made out but, for a 1000 years, scholars seemed to lose the ability to think properly. Not until the Renaissance did men start to base theories on their own critical observations rather than accept, implicitly, the writings of earlier authors. The results of this latter attitude is seen in some of the preposterous natural history of the mediaeval bestiaries. Strange ideas about bird migration lasted for centuries after the Renaissance. The ancient scholars were well aware that some kinds of birds flew away in the autumn and returned during the spring, but this information was lost to later savants. They came to the conclusion that birds behaved like mammals and went into hibernation, sometimes in extraordinary circumstances. In the 18th century Dr Johnson pronounced with sonorous authority that 'swallows certainly sleep all winter. A number of them conglobulate together, by flying round and round, and then all in a heap throw themselves under water, and lie in the bed of a river.' Dr Johnson was a city-dweller who obtained his knowledge at least secondhand. He even admitted 'sheer ignorance' when upbraided for a simple mistake in his dictionary. Yet Gilbert White of Selbourne, who was making field studies of birds at about the same time, was unable to decide whether birds migrated or hibernated. This may have been due to his living in southern England where no spectacular migration flights are to be seen. It is unlikely that the fact of migration was a mystery to the inhabitants of remote islands and coasts where wildfowl and waders make regular landfalls. They would have seen the flocks flying southwards in autumn and back north in the spring and would not have needed much imagination to come to the conclusion that the birds were flying south to avoid the harshness of winter.

It was from observations on remote islands, lighthouses and similar places that 19th-century ornithologists developed the theory of migration. They were able to co-ordinate teams of watchers at various points and show the direction and timing of migratory movements. The development of bird ringing in the 20th century gave a great impetus to the study of migration. The movements of individuals could be plotted so that a picture of each species' migration route could be built up and the location of their winter quarters discovered. Since World War II, radar has enabled ornithologists to watch the movements of migrants as they are actually taking place and even to follow the course of single birds.

Thus, it is now a commonplace that birds migrate. In temperate regions, like the British Isles, everyone knows that swallows, swifts and cuckoos 'fly to Africa' for the winter. Many people notice the arrival of fieldfares and redwings in the autumn. What is less well known is that some individuals of resident species, like robins, blackbirds, lapwings and tits also migrate. This is called partial migration. The idea that birds migrate to warmer climates to escape a shortage of food in winter is also well established as general knowledge. Yet even specialists do not properly understand why some species migrate and others do not, or how the birds know when and where to migrate. The means of navigation is also far from fully understood. In fact, the more that migration is studied, and it is receiving the attentions of many ornithologists, the more complex the problems are found to be.

There is no doubt that the prime function of migration is to allow a species to utilize a temporary abundance of food. In northern countries this means that birds move in during the warm summer months and make use of the abundant animal and plant food to raise their families. As autumn sets in, food becomes increasingly scarce and many birds are forced to travel to warmer countries. The classic example is the swallow, a familiar harbinger of spring, which, like other members of its family, feeds on flying insects caught on the wing. During the winter these insects virtually disappear and the survival of swallows in temperate regions is quite impossible. Ringing has shown that European swallows migrate to South Africa, where warm summer conditions prevail during the European winter.

The number of birds a region can support naturally depends to a large extent on its geograph-

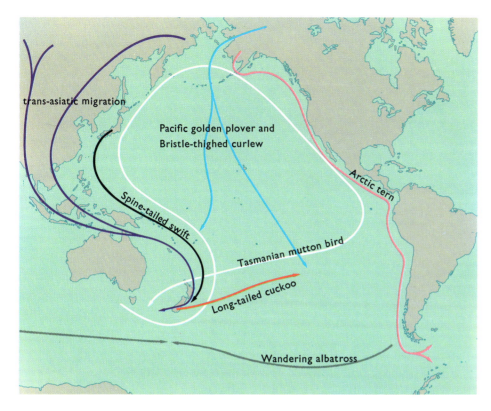

There are several outstanding migrations undertaken across the Pacific Ocean. For the Wandering albatross that nests on sub-antarctic islands there is a dispersal after the breeding season. The prevailing wester-lies carry the birds around the world but there is no particular winter home and there is no seasonal exploitation of two different habitats as there is in true migration because the albatross can feed at the same latitude all the year round. For the Long-tailed cuckoo and the Pacific golden plover the migrants have to find their second homes on certain small islands set in the vast ocean. The Spine-tailed swift has to cross the equator as the insects it feeds on only occur in regions where it is warm all the year round.

ical latitude. The British Isles, for example, sup-ports about 180 resident species and a further 55 are summer visitors that migrate away before winter. In Greenland, there are less than 30 resident species but this figure is doubled during the summer as birds flock in to exploit the short-lived abun-dance of food. Long-eared and Snowy owls, falcons and skuas come northwards to prey on small mam-

The migration routes of the White stork. The details have been worked out by ringing and direct observation. At the end of March the storks fly north, entering southern Eur-ope by the two shortest cros-sings, the Straits of Gibraltar and the Bosphorus. To cross the sea they soar high on thermals then glide to the opposite shore. After nesting the storks return to Africa with their young.

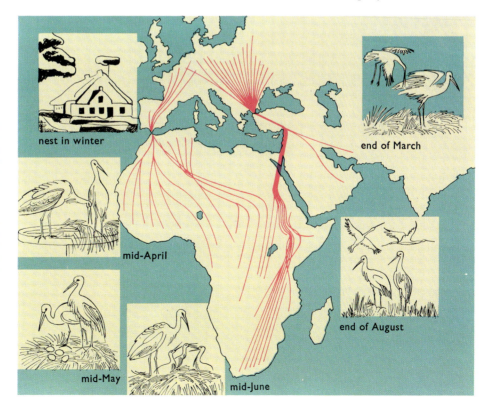

mals and birds. Fieldfares spend the summer in the tundra of northern Europe and migrate south and west in the autumn to temperate parts where they can find berries on trees and where the ground is not too frozen to probe for insects.

Record Migrants. The Arctic tern holds the record for long distance migration. It breeds around European coasts from northern France to the high Arctic islands of Jan Mayen, Svalbard and Novaya Zemlya. It is not surprising to find that the Arctic tern leaves the far north in winter. The sea and inland waters freeze and cut off the supply of small fish, crustaceans and insect larvae. What is surprising, and extremely remarkable, is that some Arctic terns migrate to the shores and islands of the Antarctic, despite the fact that the seas of temperate Europe remain open and other Arctic terns can be seen fishing offshore there all winter. It seems that there is not a parallel shift of the whole species, so that each local population travels the same distance southward, but that the terns from the north leap-frog over those living in the south. A short leapfrog would bring them to the tropics, where the sea is never very rich in small animals, and they fly on to the Southern Ocean where, during the short Antarctic summer, there is a huge supply of small marine animals.

The journey from the Arctic to the Antarctic consists of a distance of 8,000–11,000 mi (12,870–17,700 km). The Arctic terns arrive in the Antarctic as the sea ice begins to break up and disperse, and the days become longer. They are therefore able to make use of long hours of daylight during which to feed. It is often said that the Arctic tern sees more daylight than any other bird. Those that nest beyond the Arctic Circle experience 24 hours of daylight in high summer, and the sun barely sets on their wintering grounds.

Another point of interest in the story of the Arctic tern is that it is not the only kind of tern to appear around Antarctic shores as the ice breaks up. These shores are the breeding ground of the Antarctic tern which spends the winter in sub-antarctic waters. The two species are very much alike, differing mainly in size. It is tempting to think that the Antarctic tern evolved from Arctic terns that 'forgot' to fly north in the autumn and started to breed in the south. This theory does not hold as the juveniles of the two species are different. The juvenile Antarctic tern is speckled like the South American tern, while the plainer, grey and white juvenile of the Arctic tern, resembles the juvenile

Common tern which is restricted to the northern hemisphere.

Among the rivals of the Arctic tern as record migrants are two land birds, the American golden plover, which migrates from arctic Canada to southern Brazil, and the knot, a wader which travels from northern Siberia to the East Indies. These are almost direct north–south routes which contrast with those of several seabirds whose lengthy migrations from their nesting colonies to oceanic feeding grounds by roundabout routes take advantage of prevailing winds that are used to save effort.

The simplest of prevailing wind routes is that taken by Antarctic albatrosses, such as the Wandering albatross, and their smaller relative the Giant petrel. They breed in colonies of thousands on the small islands of the Antarctic and sub-antarctic. Over the years, thousands of albatrosses and Giant petrels have been ringed on the islands of South Georgia and the South Orkneys, at the southern end of the Atlantic Ocean. Large numbers of these ringed birds have been later recovered and it has been shown that, outside the breeding season, they sweep around the world under the influence of the almost continual westerly winds in these latitudes. Whether individuals, or those from a particular colony, tend to stay in one area of ocean to feed, or whether they merely fly continuously round the world is not known.

On the other hand, it is known that some of the related shearwaters feed in restricted areas where currents and upwellings cause concentrations of food organisms. The Manx shearwater (which no longer breeds on the Isle of Man) leaves the British Isles at the end of the nesting season and flies with the prevailing trade winds to shallow water on the eastern coast of South America. The Great shearwater comes the other way. It nests on Tristan da Cunha and Gough Island, in the middle of the South Atlantic, and leaves in April. At this time of the year, the trade winds sweep towards the Caribbean. From there, the shearwater continues up the eastern seaboard of North America, past Newfoundland, and across to Europe, where it spends the summer. By September, it has started on its return trip, arriving back at the nesting grounds in November.

White storks on their nest. They regularly nest on houses ▷
and their presence is said to bring good luck. The return of
the stork to the same nest and mate has made them a
symbol of fidelity.

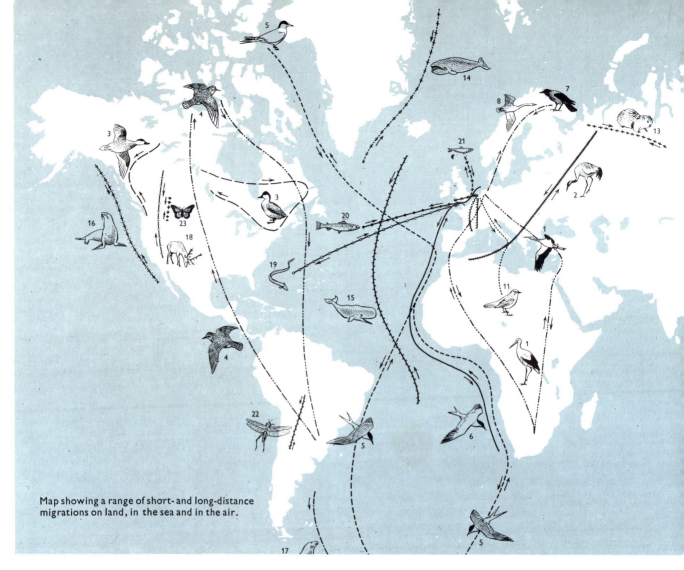

Map showing a range of short- and long-distance migrations on land, in the sea and in the air.

The routes taken by some notable bird migrants, with those of mammals, fishes and insects for comparison. Migration is most easily accomplished by flying and swimming animals as they are not hindered by geographical barriers.

Even more spectacular is the migration of the Short-tailed shearwater which nests on the shores of the Bass Strait between Australia and Tasmania. The migration route is a gigantic figure-of-eight some 20,000 mi (32,180 km) long, which carries the shearwater to the Bering Sea and back, with following winds most of the way. It first moves into the Tasman Sea, then past the Solomon Islands and up the western side of the Pacific to the Bering Sea and sometimes through the Bering Straits. On its return, it travels down the west coast of America to California and straight back across the Pacific to Australia.

Short Migrations. The spectacular transcontinental and circum-oceanic migrations draw our attention from the short distance migrations of many species. These are often interesting for reasons other than the distance involved. Some migrations are vertical and may involve no horizontal movement and the vertical component may be only a few

hundred feet, as climate changes quite rapidly with altitude. In Britain, Red grouse may move in winter from high to low moors but more well-marked vertical migrations are seen in mountainous country. The American Blue grouse migrates in the opposite direction. It spends the winter on mountains, descending in spring to eat the early buds and flowers. In India, some birds move from the Himalayas down to the plains below. In the Jordan Valley, there is a sunbird which nests 1,000 ft (300 m) below sea level and migrates to sea level or above for the winter.

The factor that affects bird life in the tropics is not coldness removing the food supply as in temperate and polar regions. Drought provides a limiting factor in the distribution of birds, and the cycle of tropical migrations is geared to the rainy season. The cycle may be quite complex. Some birds are attracted to regions where rain has brought out swarms of insects. Other birds are attracted to

1. white stork
2. crane
3. American scoter
4. American golden plover
5. Arctic tern
6. Sandwich tern
7. Hooded crow
8. Whooper swan
9. Australian swallow
10. knot
11. nightingale
12. reindeer
13. lemming
14. Greenland right whale
15. Sperm whale
16. Californian sealion
17. Sea elephant
18. wapiti
19. European eel
20. salmon
21. herring
22. locust
23. butterfly

seeds that ripen after the rains. As the rains may be local in extent the flocks become nomadic, not using a permanent route but moving about the country to take advantage of the best conditions. The Australian mistletoe-bird, one of the flower-pecker family, feeds on the berries of parasitic plants similar to the European mistletoe. Flocks of mistletoe-birds continually fly about the country in search of ripening berries and nest to coincide with the main crop.

Two species of nightjar illustrate the variety of tropical migration. Both live in the region sandwiched between the dry Sahara and the wet Zaire (Congo) forests. They move together from north to south each year. While in the north, they experience the rainy season and there the Plain nightjar lays its eggs. When they move south, where the weather is dry, conditions are right for the Standard-winged nightjar to breed.

The Hawaiian goose or né-né is peculiar because it breeds at the 'wrong' time of year – when the days are shortest. Why it should do this is not known, except that the goose comes down from the rugged lava fields to nest in the lower, lusher slopes. This reversed migration almost caused the destruction of the Hawaiian goose, which was already threatened by introduced predators. The Americans on Hawaii, very properly, kept a close season for Hawaiian geese but they did not realize the unusual timing of the breeding season and consequently shot them while they were nesting.

Stimulus for Migration. The examples of migration given in this chapter are abundant evidence of the value of migration in allowing birds to use different sources of food. What causes a bird to migrate is more difficult to explain. It does not simply migrate when food becomes scarce. Some birds migrate before there is a shortage. Furthermore, they may migrate at exactly the same time each year even though conditions of weather and food supply vary greatly. The stimulus to migrate must, therefore, be inborn; a mechanism that is passed from one generation to the next. The instinctive nature of migration is well illustrated by birds like the cuckoo in which the young migrate after the parents have left. There is no chance of their learning from their elders. It seems that a seasonal food shortage has been responsible for the evolution of migratory behaviour in a species as a whole, but the trigger that makes an individual bird leave home is a complex physiological state, depending on the bird's reproductive organs, the day length and, to a lesser extent, the weather. The ultimate importance of food is supported by the recent tendency of British blackcaps and American cardinals to remain for the winter in places where there is abundant food on bird tables.

Navigation by the Sun. For many years the problem of how migrating birds find their way has been the subject of intense experiment and speculation. If a young cuckoo, fresh out of the nest and without its parents to guide it, can migrate thousands of miles, it must have a very good navigational system. In the early days of migration study a variety of theories, many of which had little or no experimental support, were propounded to explain the marvel of migration. There was talk of a 'sixth sense' that had yet to be discovered, or making use of the Earth's magnetic field or of the Coriolis force (the force that causes bathwater to corkscrew down the plughole). It was also suggested that geographical features and the position of the sun and stars indicated to a bird its position. The trouble with all theories is that it is difficult to design experiments in which only one type of clue, for example magnetic field or the sun's position, could be given to the bird while all others were excluded. It was clear that some birds used geographical features, especially if they had had previous experience of the route. This is most noticeable in North America where there are definite migration 'flyways' along the lines of the Rockies and the Mississippi Valley. Geographical clues cannot, however, explain how the American golden plover finds its way from Alaska to Hawaii and the Marquesas Islands across the expanse of the Pacific Ocean. Nor can they explain the classic experiment in which a Manx shearwater was carried by aeroplane to Boston, U.S.A. and returned to its nest on the Welsh coast in 12½ days, a distance of over 3,000 mi (4,830 km). In such a short time it must have flown straight back yet it is very unlikely that it had ever made this particular journey before and there are no landmarks in the Atlantic.

The search for a satisfactory theory of navigation has been centred on the use of celestial clues: the sun and stars. The pioneer experiments were made by G. Kramer who kept starlings in special round cages, known now as 'Kramer cages'. As the time of migration drew near, the starlings became rest-less and fluttered against the windows or perched facing the direction in which they would have flown if they had been free to migrate. But they only did this if the sun was shining. On overcast days they did not show a preference for any direction. It was significant that the starlings allowed for the movement of the sun across the sky. To stay facing one compass direction, they had to continually alter the angle between their heading and the sun. Thus, starlings must have a mental clock, equivalent to the navigator's chronometer, which allows them to calculate the sun's compass bearing from the time of day, for example, the sun is always due south at noon.

Further experiments strengthened the 'sun position' theory of navigation. If the 'chronometer' was re-set by giving the starlings periods of artificial light and dark out of step with the sun's rising and setting, they faced the wrong way when allowed to see the sun again. They were also fooled when the apparent position of the sun was altered by placing mirrors around the Kramer cage. The use of star position by night migrants was similarly demonstrated by placing a bird in a planetarium where the position of stars could be altered.

Field experiments have given further proof of

Before migration, swallows congregate on telegraph wires and exhibit a restlessness known as *Zugenruhe*. It appears that the swallows are ready to migrate and are awaiting the signal for departure, perhaps a spell of settled weather or a change in temperature.

Often acclaimed as the champion migrant, the Arctic tern *Sterna paradisaea* migrates from the high Arctic to the sub-antarctic islands and fringes of the Antarctic continent. The round trip may involve a journey of 22,000 mi (36,000 km). Thus the tern enjoys two summers a year.

the existence of a sun compass in a bird's senses. One ingenious tracking experiment involved liberating Adélie penguins on a flat, featureless snowfield in the Antarctic. The penguins plodded off across the snow and the observers followed their trails. While the sun was shining the penguins kept a straight course, but when the sun was obscured they wandered at random.

To migrate from the nesting area to wintering grounds and to return requires more than the ability to keep a compass bearing. Not infrequently migrants are blown miles off course by wind. If they merely kept going on a fixed bearing they would fly on a parallel course to the original and become displaced. To navigate properly, a migrant must know the position of its destination and its own position at any particular time, and it must be able to relate the two in a compass course between them. This is the basic principle of navigating a ship or an aircraft. The navigating officer takes bearings on the sun or stars with a sextant, calculates his position, plots it on a chart and relates it to the position of the destination.

G. V. T. Matthews of the Wildfowl Trust, England, has elaborated a theory in which he supposes that birds are doing just this. He suggests that within a bird's head is the equivalent of a sextant, chronometer and charts. The bird's position is calculated by the sextant equivalent, observing the movement of the sun along its arc for a short time and extrapolating along that arc to give the local noon elevation. The elevation at noon gives the latitude (90° elevation at the equator). To calculate longitude, that is east–west displacement from the destination, rather than from the arbitrary reference point at Greenwich used by a navigator, the bird uses its chronometer to compare the difference in time between noon where it is and noon at its destination (there is a difference of four minutes for every degree of longitude). The position of the destination is retained as a memory of the height of the sun at noon there.

Such a brief description hardly does justice to Dr Matthew's theory but he has shown that the idea is very plausible. It is known from studies on other facets of bird life that their eyes are sensitive enough to detect the movement of the sun across the sky, that they can measure angles accurately, as when a falcon stoops at jinking prey, and that they have an excellent time sense. Evidence is also slowly gathering that this is more than a theory and some birds do, in fact, use this method of naviga-

A flock of 5,000 knots *Calidris canutus* resting during their migration. Overcast weather that makes navigation difficult or strong adverse winds may produce heavy 'falls' of migrant birds. Unless there is food available, a delay in the migration can be fatal as valuable reserves are used up.

tion, but there are also some odd facts now coming to light.

The search for experiments that show, unequivocally, that a bird is using a particular piece of information to direct its flight are continuing and they show that a single theory of navigation is not sufficient. Experiments more sophisticated than those with Kramer cages have proved homing pigeons can orientate with the aid of the sun. In one such experiment pigeons were trained to peck at a recording switch when facing home but not to peck when facing away from it. They were taken to various places around their home and, with only the sun as a clue, they pecked at the switch when facing the right direction. When the sun was hidden the pigeons failed the tests. This experiment only shows that pigeons *can* use the sun to navigate. It does not prove that this is the only means of navigation because other clues were eliminated. Another experiment has shown that, at times, they can apparently use another sense. Homing pigeons were fitted with spectacles of frosted glass and

released some distance from home. They arrived safely although they could not see the sun properly. This astonishing result confirms observations that pigeons can get home in overcast conditions even though they are unwilling to take-off. It seems that the sun is main cue for homing but there are other possibilities. This is perhaps not surprising when one considers the movements of other animals. For instance, we use our eyes to move about the house, but, if the lights have failed we can stumble from room to room with the aid of touch and hearing. As so often happens in biology, it is not possible to present a simple picture of an animal's behaviour. One cannot say 'birds navigate by the sun'. It is necessary to qualify the statement by explaining that it is known that some birds have the ability to use the sun. How they do so is not fully understood and other methods are also used.

Other Means of Navigation. The use of a magnetic compass by birds has been disputed for many years. The early experiments consisted of trying to alter the magnetic field around a bird by hanging a

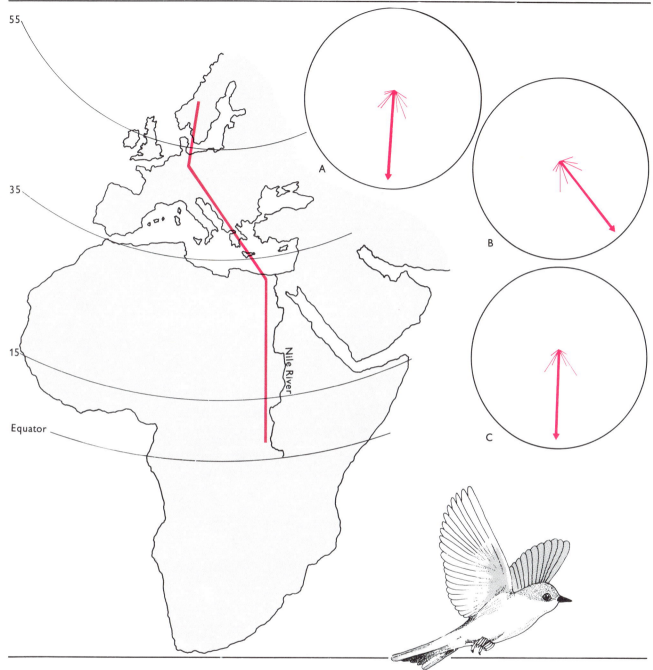

The Lesser whitethroat migrates from Scandinavia to the Nile valley each autumn along the route shown in red. Experiments show that navigation along this route is achieved with the aid of stars. A Lesser whitethroat was kept in a cage in a planetarium while the night sky was projected above it. When the projection simulated the autumn night sky seen from a latitude of 55° north, most of the whitethroat's attempts to fly were directed in a southerly direction (A). When the projection simulated the sky seen from 35° north, the whitethroat tried to fly in a south easterly direction (B), and again in a southerly direction when the projection simulated the sky seen from 15° north (C). In each case, the direction in which the bird tried to fly, corresponded with the direction which it would have taken on its journey to the Nile valley.

magnet around its neck or by placing it in a large magnetic coil. These procedures had no effect on the bird's orientation and the idea was rejected. Recently, positive results have come from German scientists who noticed that robins had continued to flutter, like Kramer's starlings, against the south-west wall of their cage after nightfall, with the blinds drawn. They then built a steel box and the robins fluttered about at random inside it. However, when the steel door was opened they took up their

The Yellow wagtail *Motacilla flava* spends the winter in Africa south of the Sahara and in Southern Asia, a few reaching Australia. It is also the only wagtail to extend into North America. It appears that Yellow wagtails have benefited from the clearance of forests as they spend the winter on airfields, golf courses and other open spaces that were once covered by tropical vegetation. There are 20 or more geographical races of the Yellow wagtail. They intermix on the wintering grounds but separate as they depart northwards. Those that breed in warmer countries leave before those going to the cooler north. Although the northern races have farther to travel, their delayed departure ensures that they arrive at the breeding grounds when there are sufficient insects on which to raise their families.

positions at the south-west wall again. The effect of the steel box was to reduce the Earth's magnetic field by about one third. It had not been eliminated entirely and after a few days the robins started to reorientate themselves. It seems from this experiment that magnetic cues cannot be sensed immediately, as can the position of the sun, but that they have a gradual effect. Since then, further experiments have been made with magnetic coils forming a magnetic field around birds. If the birds are given time to readjust it is found that their orientation can be altered by shifting the magnetic field around them.

The value of a magnetic sense to a migrating bird is that it can navigate by 'dead reckoning'

when it is unable to take sights of the sun and stars. Once again, there is a parallel with the human navigator who sails by dead reckoning in bad weather. This would explain why some migrants prefer not to travel when the weather is bad but can keep on course if overtaken by clouds. By following a magnetic compass course they can keep travelling and can correct their heading when the weather clears.

Fuel for the Journey. If the pilot of an aircraft confined his preflight calculations to navigation he would deserve to find himself paddling across the sea in a dinghy. He must check that there is sufficient fuel for the intended flight. Migrating birds, too, have to ensure that their food reserves are adequate for long periods of flight. If they are insufficient the bird dies. Overland migrants can often replenish their food reserves but many birds habitually migrate over long stretches of sea. The American golden plover has no chance of obtaining food between Alaska and Hawaii. A flight across the Pacific Ocean of 2,000 mi (3,220 km) is an extreme case but there are two non-stop flights that are carried out each year by millions of small birds. These are the crossing of the Gulf of Mexico by North American birds and the crossing of the Sahara desert by European birds. Both crossings have been studied with a view to seeing how the birds fulfil the necessary fuel requirements.

Except where they cross the Straits of Gibraltar, travel down through Italy or pass through Asia Minor, migrants heading for Africa have to cross 200–300 mi (322–483 km) of sea before coming to the Sahara. The coastal strip provides them with a chance to recuperate before the most severe stage, which is the crossing of about 900 mi (1,450 km) of desert. A desert has one advantage and one drawback over a sea crossing. The drawback is that the dry heat of the desert air increases the drain on the birds' fluid supplies and the advantage is that, even

if winds are contrary, thermals will carry the birds up and reduce the energy required to keep them airborne.

A bird's range, like that of an aircraft, is limited by the amount of fuel it can lift at take-off. The fuel used by birds for long distance flight is fat. Fat has a great advantage over carbohydrate because the latter has to be stored in chemical combination with water. To release a given amount of energy requires eight times as much carbohydrate as fat. Migrant birds put on weight rapidly before they depart. Analyses have shown that the increase is due to a heavy deposition of fat that sometimes amounts to over 50 per cent of the total body weight in small birds. At the end of a sea crossing all the fat may be used up, but the birds can put on weight again as soon as they find a feeding ground. Some calculations have been made as to the rate at which birds burn fuel in flight. It appears that small birds, such as warblers, use about 0.5 per cent of their body weight for each hour of flight. They fly at about 25–30 mi (40–48 km) per hour while migrating, and the crossing of the Sahara would take about 50–60 hours, depending on the wind. A fuel supply equal to 50 per cent of the body weight would,

The Red-backed shrike *Lanius collurio* nests in western Europe and migrates to eastern and southern Africa. The migration is known as a 'loop migration' as the northward and southward journeys take different routes. The shrikes cross the Mediterranean to land west of Egypt in the autumn and return through the Levant and Asia Minor in the spring.

155

therefore, be quite adequate for the journey. Birds that failed to find sufficient food before migrating would probably perish, particularly if they were delayed by head winds or bad weather. The advantage of possessing a 'dead reckoning' system of navigation, such as a magnetic sense, becomes very clear. The migrant can keep going and avoid suffering a fatal delay through bad weather.

Once it is realized that a bird's flight range depends not on the absolute amount of fuel carried but on the proportion of fuel to body weight, it is easy to see that there is nothing too extraordinary about small birds flying long distances. Even the tiny Ruby-throated hummingbird regularly migrates across the Gulf of Mexico, needing only 0·07–0·1 oz (2–3 gms) of fat to make the crossing. If it was not for the effect of adverse winds, very small migrants would have an advantage over large birds, such as swans and geese. The latter could not possibly fly with 50 per cent of their weight as fat but small birds have no power to counteract contrary winds. The most efficient migrators are the medium-sized birds, for instance, the waders. The American golden plover has already been cited as an example of a long distance migrant, but another wader, the Bristle-thighed curlew, performs the same migration. The Eskimo curlew is another record holder. It breeds in Alaska and migrates to the Argentine pampas. On the way south it flies eastwards to Labrador and Newfoundland where it feeds on ripening crowberries before setting off down the Atlantic seaboard to South America. It puts on so much weight by stuffing itself with crowberries that the New England settlers nicknamed it the 'doughbird'. When shot, its breast split open on hitting the ground to reveal a thick layer of dough-like fat. Unfortunately, so many Eskimo curlews were killed as they passed over New England that they disappeared for many years and were thought to have become extinct. Luckily, a few have been seen in recent years.

Hibernation. At the beginning of this chapter scorn was poured on Dr Johnson's views on the winter habits of swallows. In dismissing the notion of swallows surviving several months immersion in water as ridiculous, the baby has been thrown out with the bath water. The whole idea of hibernation of birds was for a long time regarded as impossible. Yet it would not be the first time that scientists have dismissed an old story as fable only to find later that it contained at least a germ of truth. Gilbert White's dilemma over the rival claims of migration and hibernation was well founded. He recorded a very convincing account of hibernation. A clergyman friend told him that 'when he (the clergyman) was a boy, some workmen in pulling down the battlements of a church tower early in the spring, found two or three swifts among the rubbish, which seemed at their first appearance, dead; but, on being carried towards the fire, revived. He told me that, out of his great care to preserve them, he put them in a paper bag, and hung them by the kitchen fire, where they were suffocated.'

These are well documented reports by worthy men but, to effect a radical change in scientific thought, brass-bound, watertight evidence is required. It was not until 1946 that hard proof of bird hibernation was found. In December of that year Professor E. C. Jaeger and two students found a torpid poor-will, a species of nightjar, lying in a rock crevice in the Colorado Desert. The poor-will showed no signs of life when handled, except to open one eye as it was put back in its crevice. Twice more that year Professor Jaeger returned to find the poor-will still in the crevice. The following year he returned and, again, he found the same, or another, poor-will and was able to show that it was properly hibernating over a period of 85 days.

So it is now permissible to state that birds can hibernate. The question now is how many hibernate? Hibernation has been reported for nightjars, swifts, swallows, rails and gamebirds, although proof is only accepted for the poor-will. It is known that hummingbirds become torpid at night, dropping their body temperatures from 100–57°F (38–14°C). Young European swifts, and adult White-throated swifts, are known to become torpid in bad weather when food is scarce. A second question is: given that a species has the power of hibernation, how frequently does hibernation occur? Is it just the odd individual that stays behind to hibernate while its fellows migrate? If this is the case, it would explain why so few hibernating birds are found. These questions cannot be answered because there is so little information available. We shall have to rely on chance discovery of hibernators to slowly increase our knowledge of the role of hibernation in birds. It is clear that a methodical search will not be very rewarding as it seems that hibernating birds tuck themselves deep into crevices where they are hard to find.

Index

Italics are used for generic and specific names and also to indicate pages on which illustrations appear.

Index

Italics are used for generic and specific names and also to indicate pages on which illustrations appear.